MAKING THE
BRAIN
BODY
CONNECTION

A playful guide to releasing mental,
physical & emotional blocks to success

SHARON PROMISLOW
ILLUSTRATIONS BY CATHRINE LEVAN

Kinetic Publishing Corporation
1401-1238 Seymour Street,
Vancouver B.C., Canada V6B 6J3
Ph (604) 682-8192   Fax (604) 696-6276
email: info@enhancedlearning.com

Brain Gym®, the Three Dimensions of Learning, Hook Ups, Positive Points, The Rocker, The Energizer, The Owl, The Thinking Cap, The Alphabet 8s, The Cloverleaf, Brain Organization Profiles, the brain bug graphic, and the concept of the visual midfield are all registered trademarks and copyrights of the Educational Kinesiology Foundation, and are used here with permission. For information write P.O. Box 3396, Ventura, CA 93006-3396 or call 1-800-356-2109

Parts of section 3: "Identifying the Obstacles", first appeared in *The Top Ten Stress Releasers,* © 1994, 1996 Sharon Promislow, Enhanced Learning & Integration Inc.

Canadian Cataloguing in Publication Data

Promislow, Sharon, 1943-

  Making the brain/body connection

  Revised ed.

Includes bibliographical references and index.

ISBN 0-9681066-3-3

 1. Mind and body. 2. Health. 3. Self-actualization (Psychology). 4. Mind and body therapies.

I. Levan, Cathrine II. Title.

QP388.p76 1998   *613*   *C-98-901126-4*

US Edition 1999
Canadian Edition 1998

© *1999,1998 Sharon Promislow*

Enhanced Learning & Integration Inc.
#1401–1238 Seymour Street, Vancouver BC, V6B 6J3
Third Printing 2003

Printed & Bound in Canada

Dedication

All my love to my family: Barry for his patience and support; Sean for his constant inspiration and computer smarts; Elana for her light-hearted cartoon style upon which we expanded for this book; Eric, Judy, Aimee, Daniel and especially Sarah for enriching my life.

I gratefully acknowledge my colleagues who helped turn this book into a reality: Michael Delory for the draft edition format: Cathrine Levan, whose unfailing optimism, computer kicking and editing skills, helped push this project to the finish line. In so doing, she unveiled yet another of her many talents by creating the terrific cartoons and illustrations; Marilee Boitson, who could be hired by the Department of Natural Resources after all the time she spent pulling me out of the trees so I could see the forest. Without her vision, gentle guidance and editing, this book would be longer yet, and half as clear; Blair McDonald for the fresh new format, and to my friend and colleague, Joy Ridenour, for her support and hot fax line.

Acknowledgments

Although synthesized from a variety of Educational and Specialized Kinesiology disciplines, the concepts and activities in this book owe a particular debt to Educational Kinesiology and the work of Gail Dennison & Paul Dennison, PhD. Their insights into learning through movement, the learning process itself, improved sensory processing, noticing, and the true meaning of education, provide a major inspiration for this work.

Carla Hannaford, PhD, author of *Smart Moves* was generous with her time, wisdom and emails, answering many questions regarding the neurophysiology of Brain Gym® and movement. So too, Rose Fischer-Peirick, ND, DC, never got tired of my questions. Wayne Topping, PhD, author of *Success Over Distress*, and creator of Wellness Kinesiology, continued his long-time tradition of mentoring with his unending support and sharing of materials. Thanks Wayne!

I am also deeply grateful to: Daniel Whiteside, Gordon Stokes and Candace Callaway, creators of Three In One Concepts, who brought new insight and power to the art of stress management, learning enhancement and the self-responsibility model; Eric Jensen, author of *Brain–Based Learning & Teaching,* for helping me put my kinesiology knowledge into the framework of Brain-Based Learning and State Management, and for opening a new door for my facilitation of learning: John Thie, DC, who began it all, by making laymen aware of what they could do to keep their bodies aligned, with his seminal work, *Touch For Health.*

A heartfelt thank-you to my colleagues who took the time to give feedback and encouragement at various stages of the editing process, hopefully eliminating the oops! factor. I gratefully acknowledge in alphabetical order: Carol Anne Bickerstaff, Pamela Curlee, Gail Dennison & Paul Dennison, PhD, Yvette Eastman, Rose Fischer-Peirick, ND, DC, Carla Hannaford, PhD, Eric Jensen, Kenneth Kline, Marilyn Lugaro, John Maguire, Joanne MacDonald, Stephanie Mogg, Paula Oleska, Raleigh Philp, Joy Ridenour, John Thie, DC, and last but emphatically not least, Wayne Topping, PhD—plus many other friends and students whose comments have influenced me and these pages.

Concepts and activities from all these sources provide the backbone of this work. However, the synthesis is mine, clarified by the strong direction and editing skills provided by Marilee Boitson which added much richness and form to that synthesis. I thank her for generously sharing her insight and understanding of my material, and allowing me to make use of her ideas. The final interpretation is mine. Any errors (heaven forbid!) are my own.

I would also like to acknowledge you, the reader, without whom a book does not truly exist.

Sharon Promislow

TABLE OF CONTENTS

SECTION 1

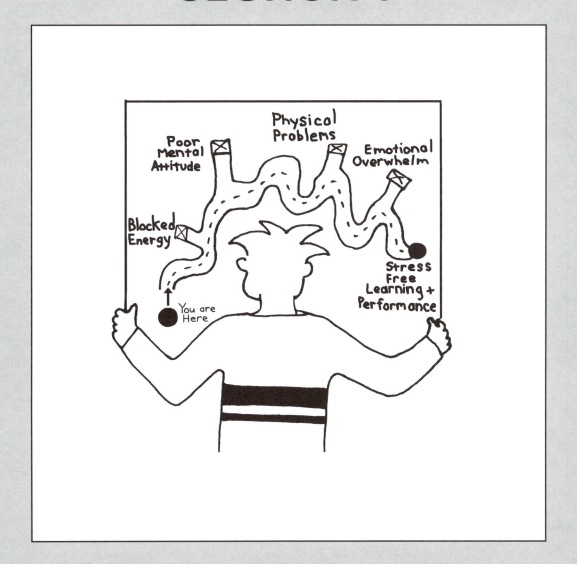

CHARTING THE COURSE

"There's no separation between the experience of the central nervous system and the function of memory in the body. The experience of the past has been fixed and retained by the neurons firing at that precise moment. Every muscle, nerve, and tissue participating in that experience has been affected and will 'remember' in its own fashion."

Gordon Stokes and Daniel Whiteside, *Tools of the Trade*, page 71

Section 1:

Charting the Course

BEFORE WE BEGIN

Although based on the most current research and theory, this book is not intended to be a weighty scientific treatise. My purpose is to have you objectively experience your response to stress, gain new insights regarding your brain/body system, and to have fun as you personally judge the efficacy of activities presented. I invite you to "do" this book as a process–not just read it.

Making the Brain/Body Connection synthesizes elements from the most up-to-date learning, brain and stress theories, with Specialized Kinesiology, into a user-friendly model for effective personal change and state management.

I have chosen to simply speak of the brain/body system, rather than engage in a discussion of "mind" and "consciousness," a more complex topic indeed! First things first: On the most basic level, the brain is simply (and complexly) a vital organ of the body—a part of the whole. No more and no less. However, for many years Western civilization perceived the body as separate from the brain or mind. It seems productive to reinforce the physiological truth by reconnecting the terms into one entity: "brain/body." If it better suits your understanding, you can substitute the terms "mind-body" or "system" wherever that term is used.

Matter affects mind, just as mind affects matter.

Many writers have addressed the issue of "mind over matter"— how our conscious intention can influence the very functioning and wellness of our body. This book also addresses the issue of the power of "matter over mind"—how re-educating the brain/body response and establishing healthy communication networks affect not only your physical body, but your learning, performance and attitude—in essence, your whole being.

As an Educational Kinesiologist, my passion is getting people to understand and improve their brain/body "hardware"—to establish and/or strengthen the neural connections for better learning and performance. My goal has always been to communicate how the brain, body and senses work, and how they can perform better for you. This book puts on paper what I love sharing, with laughter and movement, in live interaction. So you must play your part. I invite you to bring a sense of adventure and playfulness to these pages. Indeed, we are building upon developmental neural connections that were put into place in childhood, which we can deepen and refresh at any age. Share what "feels right" with family and friends. One size does fit all!

Self responsibility is key

Remember:
the only expert on you is you!
Be self-responsible!

Don't be distracted by mind chatter!

This book will introduce you to some gentle body movements designed to develop neural connections to energize you and improve the communication between your brain and body. Just remember: The only expert on you is you, and there should never be any discomfort as you do these activities. Only do them to the extent they are comfortable, and be congruent with the advice of your licensed medical practitioner. Small movements can activate the circuits as effectively as big ones; you will still notice the difference.

Handling "mind chatter"

Is there anything keeping you from being fully focused while you are reading this book? Any errands to run, kids to pick up, calls to make, etc.? STOP! Write down this "mind chatter" now, so your brain can relax and feel organized. Otherwise the brain will feel compelled to repeatedly drag up reminders from your unconscious mind at inappropriate moments, breaking your focus and concentration. If more mind chatter occurs as you are reading this book, add it to this list with the self commitment to attend to it later. Also note; this is an effective stress management technique.

Wherever you see a pencil symbol, do the Insight activity.

Mind Chatter: Things I have to remember to do later
❑ _____
❑ _____
❑ _____
❑ _____
❑ _____
❑ _____

HOW DO I USE THIS BOOK?

A s Cole Porter once said, "Anything Goes!" Scan the book right side up. Scan the book upside down. Read the theory sections, or go straight to the Balancers. Read the contents at the front of each section, and prime your brain by asking a few questions. Learn the Quick Six on pages 36-38 before you read the text. Go for a walk between chapters. Just look at the pictures. Process the whole book from front to back. Focus on the issue currently affecting you. Do the personal insight activities. Have a snack. Do the goal setting first. Highlight your favorite parts. Write notes in the columns. Explore and share your own good ideas. Turn down important pages. Read it aloud with a friend. The only thing you must not do, is to place this book on a shelf and ignore it. It will whimper until you play with it.

Read this book back to front or upside down. Mark it up. Maybe you can even balance it on your head for better posture.

Let it be a moving experience

The activities in *Making the Brain/Body Connection* are meant to be experienced with all your senses. Don't just read them, do them! You get much deeper results by moving, doing and participating, than by simply reading or listening.

Get some personal insight

Take the time to thoughtfully complete the insight activities in the book. By consciously identifying your current functioning and by setting specific goals when requested, you gain valuable conscious awareness and self knowledge of both your goals and your brain/body responses. In turn, this knowledge helps you to define areas where you would most benefit by enhancing your performance. It also allows you to notice how you feel and function in relationship to your challenges before using the brain/body balancers, giving you a baseline against which you can measure the improvement you will experience.

Take frequent breaks

Whenever your brain gets tired of the talk-talk, take a break—take a sip of water, stretch, peek ahead and play with a new brain/body activity. Do whatever you must...then return to the text refreshed. The brain was designed to cycle between acquiring new information and integrating that information into the brain/body connection. Brain research indicates that we are able to concentrate on learning new information for as many minutes as we are years old, to a maximum of twenty. So take frequent breaks, and see page 174 for more hints on stress-free learning!

ACTIVITY KEYS

Look for these symbols to prompt your processing!

Insight Activity: Honestly answer the questions in each insight box to heighten self perception into your behavior and level of current functioning.

Pre-check Activity: Notice how you feel and function before using the Brain/Body Balancers, to give yourself a baseline against which you can measure your improvement.

Brain/Body Balancer: An activity that restores brain/body integration, unlocks stuck energy, and supports easeful, optimal functioning.

Post-check Activity: A repeat of your pre-check activity so you can notice improvements in your performance and ease of functioning, making your brain/body re-education more permanent.

Quick Six Activity: One of the six powerful self management balancers listed on pages 36-38, that can be utilized anytime, anywhere, without attracting undue attention. Together, they restore a balanced, focused state.

INTRODUCTION

Meet the most marvellous operating system of all–your own brain/body

Every day new advances in technology are trumpeted– computers that run faster, have more sophisticated operating systems, process more complicated tasks with ease, have more desktop RAM, more hard drive capacity, and communicate better with other systems.

It's amazing to think that the same people who invest time, energy and money in acquiring and learning how to operate these technological miracles, will forget that their own brain/body system is the most sophisticated example of integrated functioning that exists on this planet—light years beyond the most sophisticated technology.

We all want to enjoy more productivity, creativity, health and well-being. On that note, are you willing to invest a few moments to discover some simple, holistic principles of your brain/body's operation? Are you willing to learn a few simple activities to assure its highest functioning? Are you willing to simply (emphasis on the simply) get better? No special materials are necessary. You already possess all that you need in your own being and in the palms of your hands!

The good thing about "losing it" is...it feels good when you find it again!

When we "lose it"

You're a student, professional or an athlete, well prepared for your exam, meeting, or game. You know your stuff, and then...just when it counts–on the test, in front of the audience, on the field... you blank out, forget the answers, lose your focus and, literally or metaphorically, drop the ball.

What is it that keeps us from being the best we can be? What is blocking us from being more creative, realizing our goals and achieving success in our personal and professional lives?

Put simply, as soon as we get stressed our brain/body integration breaks down, leaving us learning and living "disabled" and /or

Under any kind of stress, brain integration breaks down, and it becomes difficult to do and think at the same time.

disconnected. Many behavioral and learning problems, such as blanking out during a test when you knew the answers five minutes beforehand, typify this dis-integration.

When we are under stress, energy for the brain areas of higher cortical reasoning can be blocked, communication between the left and right brain hemispheres can break down, and sensory organs (eye, ear, etc.) can involuntarily "switch off." We revert to a dominant brain organization pattern geared for our survival, which cuts off access to the non-dominant brain and senses. It then becomes difficult to do and think at the same time. Everything requires more effort, and stress levels increase further. We need to free that stuck energy and re-establish communication in order to integrate our brain/body system and perform optimally.

Fortunately, there is an effective answer. It has been my experience as a Specialized Kinesiologist working in both the educational and corporate communities, that the same techniques that help support the learning challenged child to read, can be used to help us all perform and function better.

Blocks to our success are caused by interference to optimal brain/body communication. *Making the Brain/Body Connection* will teach you to recognize how and where interference is occurring, then give you the tools from Specialized Kinesiology to remove that interference. These skills will enable you to release the mental, physical and emotional blocks that sabotage your best efforts, or at the very least clearly pinpoint areas of weakness where specific additional professional support is needed.

What is "brain/body integration?"

The moebus strip is a perfect metaphor for brain/body communication.

When we are functioning at our best, clear messages feed from all parts of the body to the brain and back again to the body in a loop. Sensory data is processed in an integrated fashion throughout the brain and intentional action is easy. Have you played with the mathematical concept of a moebus strip? Take a strip of paper, give it a half twist before you tape the ends together, and you end up with a loop which has no beginning or end, with both sides flowing continuously front to back. This is a good metaphor for the relationship of optimal **brain/body** functioning. Clear communication on a body level is a precursor to our ability to have clarity of thought and expression in our intellectual life.

What is a "state?"

A **state** is a "mind-body moment" and is made up of our thoughts, our feelings and our physiology, including our eye movements, breathing patterns, posture and gestures, state of health and physical comfort.[1] A state can change instantaneously, as soon as you change any of the variables.[2]

Take a moment to imagine yourself in front of a blazing fire, feet up, good music, nice refreshment a hand's reach away. Ahhhh! Now vividly imagine being in the middle of rush hour traffic, horns honking, hands gripping the steering wheel, adrenaline surging as you attempt to change lanes. Notice the difference in your thinking, feeling and physical being (your state) in the instant that you change your thoughts!

Educational researchers have termed that the ideal learning state requires a state of consciousness known as "flow," an uninterrupted state in which one "loses oneself" in the performance, a timeless, pleasure producing absorption in the experience. Eric Jensen sums it up nicely: When your skills, attention, environment and will are all matched up with the task, you are "in the flow." It's the perfect combination of your personal skill level increasing at the same time that the challenge of the task seems to increase.[3]

If we are to be physically well, mentally alert and productive as well as emotionally balanced, we must know how to achieve and maintain this balanced, positive state. Specialized Kinesiology provides a wonderful new perspective on the science and art of state management. We will give you a hands on grasp of how state management is not just an activity of mind: It's a whole brain/body experience, putting you in the flow from head to toe!

State Bound does not necessarily mean you're going to California.

What is Specialized Kinesiology?[4]

Kinesiology is defined as the study of the body in movement. Specialized Kinesiology teaches simple yet profound techniques for switching on the brain/body connection to enhance functioning. This field of study synthesizes principles and techniques from Applied Kinesiology, Acupressure, energy theory, current brain research, stress management, Neuro Linguistic Programming, chiropractic and body work, into an open-ended energy based model for re-educating the body's neural response to stress.

Specialized Kinesiologists look at how muscles, movement and posture can affect and also reflect change within the body systems themselves. We use that information to pinpoint where we need improvement, and after balancing activities, to confirm we have achieved it. Compared to the medical model which responds to symptoms, we choose instead to concentrate exclusively on restoring natural energy flow and movement to the body, and releasing the classic stress response. When muscle checking is used, it is not measuring the strength of a muscle itself, but rather evaluating the nervous system that controls the muscle's function.[5]

Our energy model

In the Specialized Kinesiology energy model, the fusion between physical body, mental perception and emotional feeling is holistic and complete, or in other languaging, comprises one "state of being," which in turn underlies our behavior. Change one component of the state, no matter how little, and the whole state (by necessity) transforms, allowing new possibilities of behavior. Conversely, changing the behavior can change the state. That is how seemingly miraculous shifts in learning and functioning take place with seemingly simple interventions. That is why Specialized Kinesiology works, or for that matter, why other modalities for change work.

How we acquire blocks to learning & success

How does a block impinge on our optimum state of being? Current research suggests that memory does not just live in the brain: It lives in every cell of the body. Therefore our natural tendency to acquire blocks from life events can be reduced to a simple formula:

Event + Perception + Intense Emotion = Stuck Circuit Lock[6]

Events in themselves are neutral. However, when we experience an event, we humans filter it through our own mental perceptions, then color it with our own meaning and emotion as part of our innate reaction. For example: You are walking down the street and a snarling dog lunges toward you. Gasp! You perceive danger.

When we experience a trauma, the position of our body plus everything we are feeling thinking, seeing and hearing becomes locked into a circuit.

Your heart starts pounding and you experience fear. All the neural circuits firing at the time of the perception of danger—the exact position of your body, the muscles that were being used, the direction of your eyes and especially the emotions you felt and your reaction (freeze? run?) during that event become fused into a circuit of cellular memory. It doesn't matter if the dog stops short and licks your hand. From that moment on, each time you fire off any part of that circuit—use the same muscle sequence, look in the same direction, experience a similar event or feel the same emotion—you will fire off the whole sequence of reactions that was part of your survival response during that first instant you saw the dog lunge—even if the initial event has long since been forgotten. Depending on the person involved, the key by-product may be (1) a mental block or a limiting belief—"I don't like dogs" or "animals are dirty"; (2) an emotional block—"I HATE and FEAR dogs, animals, walking down the sidewalk, sudden movement toward me" or (3) a physical block —"Gosh, I have a headache, back ache, or leg cramp. Guess I can't go for a walk today!" Some people may have just one type of block, others will have all three.

Old, failed relationships can create a perceptual filter that stops us from seeing the present clearly!

We can experience positive locks as well–a happy event, infused with positive emotion leading to a positive life outlook and confidence. Occasionally this will also create expectations and optimism that are not realistic. So circuit locks can manifest as emotional patterns, positive or negative, which may need to be identified and re-educated to allow us to clearly and sensibly deal with present situations without being unrealistically colored by our past life experience.

For those of us who work with computers, a fitting metaphor is to compare life to a drawing program where you can do overlays that you then lock into place to form a final picture. Change the details of any of the overlays [i.e. the color of the background], and you end up with a different picture. A micro intervention can make a macro difference!

Meet some simple energy switches

The "buttons and switches" taught in this book all work to release stuck circuit locks in the brain/body. Using these energy switches can restore the normal, unstressed flow of energy and brain/body messaging, at the same time stimulating other important body systems—the lymphatic system, the neurovascular system, our central nervous system to name but a few. The first "energy switch" we will speak to is simple movement.

Movement: As we will explore in much more detail later, body movement stimulates the "feel good" chemical messengers of our system. Endorphins are the natural opiate manufactured by the body, and production is stimulated by movement, as the famous runner's "high " confirms. Slow cross-lateral movement stimulates the manufacture of dopamine in the frontal lobe of the brain (affecting our ability to see patterns and to learn faster), in the limbic area (controlling our emotions) and in the basal ganglion (intentional movement). This is one of the neurotransmitters for which millions of children, diagnosed as ADD or ADHD, take Ritalin to balance. The educational implications are staggering. We can use targeted body movement and natural process to help enhance the manufacture, balance and transportation of informational substances (and the flow of subtle balanced energy) in the body.

Touch For Health Energy Switches: Some of the key methods drawn from the Touch for Health synthesis include Neurolymphatic Reflex Points, Neurovascular Holding Points, Meridian Energy tracing and Spindle Cell Reflex Release. All these techniques are accessing and working with surface subtle energy systems, which in turn access and impact other interconnected systems, releasing energy blocks on deeper levels.

Neurolymphatic Reflexes[7]: The lymphatic system is the body's recycling system, designed to gather up dead cells, waste from the cells and excess water, and to carry them to the bloodstream. Neurolymphatic reflexes (nerve stimulation points enhancing lymph flow) were discovered and mapped out in the 1930's by an osteopath named Frank Chapman. He related these reflexes to disturbances in the glandular and organ systems. Later Dr. George Goodheart, a chiropractor, correlated these reflexes to specific muscles, and discovered that stimulating these reflexes can also release energy blocks and stress to the muscles, improving their strength. Proper diet and exercise are also important for enhancing lymphatic flow.

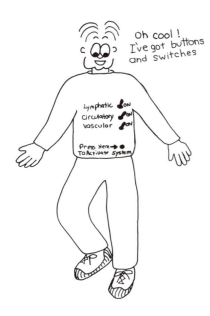

Learn all about the buttons and switches of your body with Specialized Kinesiology.

The neurolymphatic reflexes are points located mainly on the chest in the rib spaces next to the breast bone, and on the back along the spine, and are stimulated through rubbing in a circular motion with the fingers. You will be introduced to a few key ones in this book. When we ask you to massage a spot, it's a good bet you'll be rubbing a neurolymphatic reflex point!

Neurovascular Holding Points[8]: These were discovered by Dr. Terrance Bennett, DC, also in the 1930's. Located mainly on the head, when held lightly with a slight upward stretch, these neurological switches redirect blood flow to their related muscle organ or gland.[7] Positive Points on page 85 are a good example!

Meridian Energy and Acupressure Points[9]: As we will discuss in more detail on page 55, body energy has been charted as flowing in specific pathways we call meridians. There are acupuncture points along the meridians, electromagnetic in character, almost like signalling towers of a transmitting system to specific organs, muscles and functions. When there is a blockage, we can hold acupressure points, or, as we will do later in this book with Gait Reflex Points, we will rub acupressure points on the feet to stimulate energy flow throughout the body. Acupuncture stimulates the release of endorphins to create analgesia (pain relief), and acupressure massage can reap the same rewards.

Muscle Spindle Cell Reflex Technique[10]: The spindle cell is a specialized nerve cell which senses position and tension within a muscle and which monitors the muscle's length and the rate of change in its length. We will use this mechanism to experiment with the efficiency of our brain/body communication. The technique is also valuable to relax muscles when they cramp.

We can unlock our blocks to success with gentle process.

In summary: We work backwards from identifying the physiological locks–both obvious and subtle–that underlie our blocks to success. Once identified, we use energy switches and gentle process to unlock emotion, perception and physical reaction to the original event. Not until we consciously learn to objectively identify our stress reactions and re-educate our neural response to the original stimuli, are we free to experience better solutions and actions.

Although this book creates artificial divisions into logical teaching modules (such as electromagnetic, emotional, motor and sensory balancers), the reality is you may improve your eyes using electromagnetic balancers; you may improve your emotional state by changes in physical posture and nutrition; you may improve your digestion by rubbing your ears, etc. Any switch can be the key release point of an energy blockage, the release of which reinstates normal flow and higher functioning to the whole system, even seemingly unrelated areas.

What results can I expect?

What results do you want? One of the first things we will have you do is to define where you personally want improvement. We invite you to have high expectations. Just because the process is easy doesn't mean you won't experience profound shifts in your personal effectiveness as a result of this book.

Anything you do becomes easier when you identify and re-educate your blocks.

Depending upon your personal starting point, look for relaxation, higher energy, more easeful seeing, hearing, writing and learning. All you need to bring to this book is a willingness to mix and match the activities that work for you, and a commitment to use them! Look for a higher level of brain/body integration which can bring a new ease and insight to everything you do and learn, be it as a student, professional, athlete, artist or life adventurer.

Interestingly, many individuals using these methods have reported relief from chronic pain. The brain/body is designed to protectively shut down power to damaged areas, and sends messages of pain to keep us from using that area which needs time to heal. Sometimes after the healing is complete, the brain circuitry does not switch back to normal flow and we must re-educate the "stuck" pain circuit.

Breakthroughs in sports performance are common, as are sometimes astonishing improvements in academic and work performance. The bottom line is that in the absence of gross pathology, incredible change can occur quickly by identifying and re-educating these "stuck" behavioral and functional locks.

This book is intended to provide simple tools for handling any stress in the moment, and for identifying the currently associated energy blockages which may impede you. This book is not intended to permanently address all the "ins and outs" of a human life in two seconds or less. Major issues may require professional attention, be it from a Specialized Kinesiologist, a counsellor or licensed medical professional. However, these activities can provide a wonderful first step into self management, self control and ultimately, self esteem. The same way that you wouldn't expect just one bath to keep you sweet smelling for a lifetime, it is in your best interest to develop a pattern of regularly using the techniques we are about to offer in these pages.

This book is designed as a step-by-step process in which you will:

1. Learn how your brain/body works, and how you can support it to work optimally.

2. Master a tool—Noticing—your own biofeedback mechanism for accessing how your brain/body is currently supporting or sabotaging you in achieving your goals.

3. Identify the key stressors in your life: Learn to recognize the psychological and physiological results of that stress.

4. Explore and experience how the brain, body and senses interrelate and process information—and how they can do it better.

5. Be introduced to brain/body balancers used to effect change. You will re-educate your body and central nervous system with easy-to-do techniques and body motions drawn from Specialized Kinesiology.

7. Put it all together in a model you can easily apply to identify and handle any specific learning and performance issue in your life.

Let the journey begin! No seat belts are necessary.

NOTES

SECTION 2

CHECKING THE EQUIPMENT

"...stress is not inherent in an event but results from how you perceive and, therefore, respond to the event...Therefore one key to reducing stress is to modify your perceptions. Instead of a crisis...see exactly the same situation as an opportunity."

Dr. Wayne Topping, *Success Over Distress*, p.20

Section 2:

Checking the Equipment

WHERE I AM NOW

The following insight activities will bring into conscious awareness your current experience of life issues, behaviors, goals and body response. This in turn will give you a baseline against which you can later measure your improvement. You stand to gain more benefit from this book by being ruthlessly honest, as the brain seems willing to re-educate functioning around consciously acknowledged issues and goals.

When you do the insight activities, notice how you feel and function. Later, after doing the brain/body balancers, check again to note improvement!

Insight: My current negative issues and behaviors

Check the box next to any issue or behavior that is current for you. Check twice if especially evident.[1]

❏ Accident prone
❏ Argumentative
❏ Clumsy
❏ Daydream
❏ Deadline stress
❏ Difficulty concentrating
❏ Difficulty following directions
❏ Difficulty giving directions
❏ Difficulty making decisions
❏ Difficulty telling time
❏ Disorganized
❏ Disturbing to others
❏ Do not handle stress well
❏ Do not enjoy exercise
❏ Easily distracted
❏ Excitable
❏ Fight
❏ Hearing difficulties
❏ Impatient
❏ Impulsive
❏ Lack confidence

❏ Lack creativity
❏ Learning difficulties
❏ Leave projects incomplete
❏ Letter or number reversals
❏ Long walks cause discomfort
❏ Over-active
❏ Poor eye/hand coordination
❏ Poor handwriting
❏ Poor reading comprehension
❏ Poor sports performance
❏ Poor time management
❏ Procrastination
❏ Reading difficulties
❏ Restless/fidgety
❏ Rub eyes a lot
❏ Slow in completing work
❏ Stress headaches
❏ Stop in middle of game
❏ Talk too much
❏ Unpredictable
❏ Vision problems

The more issues your brain identifies as relevant, the more improvement you will achieve.

WHERE I WANT TO BE

At the outset, please increase the effect of this book in your life by spending a few minutes on identifying desired outcomes. As just mentioned, the brain/body tends to improve functioning about a defined intention. Therefore it is important to clearly define where you desire improved performance and functioning.

Identify your aspirations. Get clear goals- be they material or non-material.

Insight: What do you want to improve as a result of having bought this book....and why?

List areas where you want better performance and/or your specific goals.

Give three reasons it's important for you to reach or exceed the goals you listed above.

1.

2.

3.

Identify what's holding you back (check previous exercise on page 27 for inspiration!)

What do you stand to lose if you don't reach your goals?

What would change good or bad if you do?

Write them down, so they are real to you.

HOW TO MEASURE MY PROGRESS

Noticing: my biofeedback tool

How will you know which activities are most effective for you? Rather than using expensive, high tech biofeedback equipment, we advocate two no-cost, effective techniques used extensively in Specialized Kinesiology. The first is Muscle Checking—a superb means for providing biofeedback from the brain and central nervous system by testing the integrity of muscle strength and balance. The second is Noticing—developing a conscious, detailed, objective awareness of our current state of being, including posture, muscle tension, breathing patterns and sensory activity. Effective muscle checking requires training, but you can learn to Notice in ten minutes or less, starting now! We like to present Noticing as a part of an "information sandwich."

The information sandwich:

The top slice of the sandwich: First we **pre-check** how we are functioning in regard to any goal or issue and notice how effectively we are currently performing, and any stress reactions in our body. There are no rights or wrongs—just an objective recognition of our current reaction patterns and functional blockages.

The filling: We then do **integrating activity** (brain/body balancers) to release the blockage created by stress in our brain/body.

The bottom slice: the **post-check**—We repeat the Noticing process and assess our improvements in functioning as we resume pursuit of our goal or continue to deal with our issue .

If we have improved enough, our work is complete. If we are not yet satisfied, we simply repeat the balancing activities or add new ones until we achieve our desired level of enhanced performance. We can continue to evaluate our reactive patterns and our performance, repeating the sandwich as needed.

Noticing is a no-cost, effective means of biofeedback to help you recognize progress toward your goals. It is used brilliantly in Brain Gym® for educational anchoring.

How will you know if these techniques make a difference ?
Notice:
Do you feel better?
Are you more effective?
Are things easier?

THE INFORMATION SANDWICH

Notice how you are functioning

Use Integrating Activity

Notice improvement in performance

Mental Rehearsal:
As far as the brain is concerned,
when you visualize a successful
outcome in detail, you are
establishing the experiential
connections to give your brain
the confidence that you have
"been there, done that, made it
successfully to the top!"

Mind over matter

Our mental perceptions can define our physical capabilities. Scientific proof supports the idea that what we imagine is as real to our brain as what we have actually experienced. PET (Positron Emission Tomography) measuring blood flow, MRI's (Magnetic Resonance Imaging) and CAT scans (Computerized Axial Tomography) measuring chemical composition, and EEG (Electroencephalograms) measuring electrical transmission, show virtually the same brain activity for both real and imagined activity.

What does this mean to you? As far as the brain is concerned, when you visualize a outcome in detail (good or bad), you are creating the neural associations that would be stimulated by a real life experience, and triggering the same brain/body circuitry. It explains why our Noticing activities on the next pages, based on imagining a stressful issue, provide powerful insight into real life reactions. Let's experience first-hand how our shift in perception impacts our external capabilities, and how it happens instantly.

Insight: Moving beyond your limitations

Stand comfortably, looking straight ahead. Raise your right arm straight forward, at a right angle to your body. Now gently turn your head, arm and torso to your right as far as you can go without straining. Note how far you can rotate, and note a spot or object that is the furthest thing your hand is pointing to.

Face forward again with your arm down. Close your eyes and allow your whole body to relax. Imagine you are the pretzel person in a circus, capable of turning with ease, around and around. Really get the image of having the flexibility of rubber. See this as a metaphor for your mental flexibility, able to move beyond your old beliefs of limits in all your endeavours. Breathe deeply.

Raise your right arm again, and once again turn gently to the right. Note how far you can now turn and to what your arm is pointing. Did you increase your range of motion on the turn? Wow! That's the power of mental rehearsal! Repeat the process, this time turning to the left to equalize your new-found flexibility.

Now that you have experienced the power of mind over matter, we can have you experience Noticing as a tool for self evaluation.

Getting a baseline for my brain/ body's current functioning

Take a minute to do the following insight activities and record what you notice. We will explore what your findings mean in light of the stress response, in section 3.

Insight: A closer look at how my body acts and reacts when I am relaxed and comfortable.

Stand comfortably and imagine yourself in a relaxing situation. Now objectively notice what your body is doing, remembering there are no rights or wrongs, just what is. This gives you a relaxed baseline against which you can later measure your body's reaction to stress.

Notice your posture in relation to the floor. (e.g. upright, swaying forward, backwards or sideways)

Notice any tension, pain or weakness in your body. Where is it? (e.g: legs, back, shoulders, neck, stomach, chest, throat, jaw)

Notice your emotional state. How you are feeling? Excited, happy, sad, tense, motivated, withdrawn, etc?

Notice your mental state. Can you think clearly or are you confused?

Look at an object straight ahead. Is it clear or blurry?

Listen to a sound in the room. Is it tinny or resonant? Are you hearing equally through both ears?

Lift your arms 30 º up in front of your body. Is that easy or does it take effort?

Hold your arms there for 30 seconds. Is it easy or difficult?

Jot down what you feel are the most interesting aspects of your body's response to visualizing a relaxed state.

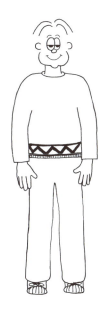

"I am lying on a beach in Hawaii, under a swaying palm tree..."

What do you notice in your body response when you imagine a relaxed scenario? If someone were to gently nudge you forward, then back, would you feel solid or wobbly? Try it!

Can you stand firm while you think of your stressor? If someone were to gently push you forward, then back, then gently nudge you to the left, and to the right, would you feel solid or wobbly? Try it!

Insight: A closer look at how my body acts and reacts under stress.

Now think of something challenging or stressful. Repeat the Noticing process and compare with your baseline of relaxation.

Stand comfortably and think of something stressful. Objectively notice what your body is doing.

Notice your posture in relation to the floor. (e.g. upright, swaying forward, backwards or sideways)

Notice any tension, pain or weakness in your body. Where is it? (e.g. legs, back, shoulders, neck, stomach, chest, throat, jaw)

Notice your emotional state. How you are feeling? Excited, sad, tense, motivated, withdrawn , etc?

Notice your mental state. Can you think clearly or are you confused?

Look at an object straight ahead. Is it clear or blurry?

Listen to a sound in the room. Is it tinny or resonant? Are you hearing equally through both ears?

Lift your arms 30 º up in front of your body. Is that easy or does it take effort?

Hold your arms there for 30 seconds. Is it easy or difficult?

Notice differences in your body reaction to the stressful situation versus the relaxed situation. Write down the most noticeable differences.

MY PERSONAL BRAIN ORGANIZATION PROFILE

Now, further insight into how we function individually. Each of us has a dominant hand: We are either right-handed or left-handed. Did you realize that we also have a dominant foot, eye, ear and brain hemisphere? When we are under stress, we revert to a very individual "default" setting, or what Brain Gym® calls our Personal Brain Organization Profile. Exploring this profile is a profound way to get insight into our stuck circuit locks, and how our brain and senses react to stress.

It's revealing to chart our Brain Organization Profile. It explains to some degree why we have experienced our life—both strengths and weaknesses—in a certain way up to this point. Once we recognize our patterns and start doing the integrating activities in this book, this pattern becomes historic. But for fun and self-recognition of your established patterns, do the Quick Test of Dominance on the next page. If you are interested in a more accurate Brain Dominance Organization Profile (which requires muscle checking), seek out a qualified Brain Gym Facilitator, or take the Brain Dominance Organization course available through the Educational Kinesiology Foundation. The balancers in this book alone can help you integrate brain and body to improve the functioning of your non-dominant hemisphere and senses.

Our dominance can change, depending on the task and our state of being.

Dr. Carla Hannaford, in her book *The Dominance Factor*, explores 32 different possible dominance patterns and their ramifications based on the original work of Dr. Paul Dennison, creator of Brain Gym. For our purposes, it suffices to say that a mixed profile, (any combination of dominant hand, eye and ear feeding into different sides of the brain) can lead to learning difficulties if the two sides of the brain are not communicating. Information is not being shared easily, nor does it have the same hemispheric orientation as you shall understand as our book unfolds. For instance, if a dominant logical eye gets its "audio feed" from a dominant whole picture ear, it can be like watching a foreign film with no subtitles, and can lead to learning problems. Other combinations also have their strengths and drawbacks.

The point of this exercise is to encourage you to do the integrating activities in this book which will allow you access to the integrated wisdom of your whole brain and all your senses, whereas in the past you were preset to perceive and express in a predetermined and perhaps limited way.

Insight: A Quick Exploration of Brain Dominance

Don't worry if you are unfamiliar with some of the terms: You will meet them all in detail in later sections. Also important. Do not have brain surgery based on your findings!

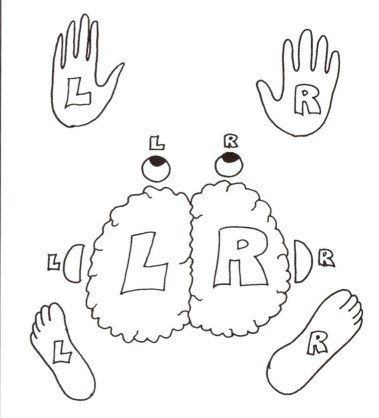

Color in your dominant senses and limbs[2.]

1. **HAND:** a. With which hand do you throw a ball? (gross motor)
   ❏ Left ❏ Right (color in the brain bug & label "gross")
   b. With which hand do you write? (fine motor)
   ❏ Left ❏ Right (color in the brain bug & label "fine")

cont. next page

2. **FOOT**: Squarely face a ball and (without thinking) lift your foot as if to kick it. Which foot did you use? ❏ Left ❏ Right (color in)

3. **EYE:** Hold your arms straight out in front of you and make a small triangle between your clasped hands to peek through at any object you choose. Close each eye and see which eye holds the image steady when the other is closed. The dominant eye will hold it steady, the non-dominant eye will shift the image. ❏ Left ❏ Right (color in Brain Bug)

4. **EAR:** Hold a piece of paper in front of you with both hands. Pretend it is a wall (or face a real wall) and imagine something fascinating is occurring on the other side. Put your ear up to the "wall" to eavesdrop. Which ear did you turn to the wall? That is your dominant ear. ❏ Left ❏ Right (color in Brain Bug)

5. The best way to determine your **DOMINANT BRAIN HEMI-SPHERE** with Noticing is to first stand up comfortably. Without thinking about it, let your weight shift onto one leg. Your dominant hemisphere is likely the one opposite to the weight bearing leg. Don't base your major career choice on this result alone! ❏ Left ❏ Right (color in Brain Bug)

6. One really can't determine with assurance through Noticing which brain hemisphere is your **DETAIL** (logic) and which is your **WHOLE PICTURE** (gestalt). A guesstimate would be to ask, "when you have three hours of free time to do what you love best, would you read a book, do a crossword puzzle, research a family tree, (more logical) or would you play a sport, paint a picture, play in a band (gestalt). Also ask yourself: Do you like to analyze, write and talk about problems (logic brain), or rather than expressing in language, do you see the whole situation, feel the emotion, and need to move (whole picture brain). That function would then live in the hemisphere opposite your weight bearing leg, as determined in #5.

I guess my dominant hemisphere is ❏ Logic ❏ Gestalt

What I find most interesting about my basic brain dominance profile:

The way you take a stand tells a lot about your dominant brain!

The picture is getting into clearer focus. You have identified some areas where you want improved functioning. You have noticed how your body reacts to stress, and are aware of how your brain patterns shift. You have triggered some stuck circuit locks. Before we go further, let's practice what we preach, and start rebalancing your brain/body response to a higher functioning level.

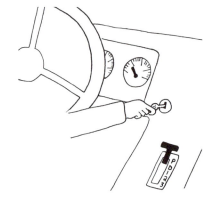

STARTING MY ENGINE WITH THE QUICK SIX

Previously in this section you noticed what happened while you thought of a challenging or stressful situation— how in an instant your "state of being" changed. Now we'll give you a first-hand experience of how simple, fast and effective the re-education process can be using the Quick Six. These activities will be more fully explained in later sections. We simply want you to experience how quickly you can create a change for the better.

The Quick Six create a calm, balanced energy state, which is an essential first step to non-resistant change, and optimum learning and performance. Think "Quick Six" as a fast fix whenever you note yourself slipping into non-serving energy or behavior patterns.

THE QUICK SIX

1. Drink Water (page 57)

Get out that water bottle! Proper hydration is essential for good health on many levels. Relating to brain/body communication, water provides the medium necessary for optimum messaging throughout the brain/body. It heightens energy, improves concentration and academic skills.

- If no medical limitation, on any given day you need to drink one 250 ml glass for every 10 kg of body weight OR one 10 oz glass for every 30 lbs of body weight.

- Plus: 1 glass for each cup of coffee or caffeinated drink.

- Plus: 2 glasses for each alcoholic beverage.

Drink Water

MORE QUICK SIX

2. Plug In for Balanced Energy (page 58)

Here's an important electromagnetic quick fix to balance disturbances to the body's electrical signalling system. Place the fingertips of one hand around the navel. At the same time:

1. Massage under the collarbone, both sides of sternum.

2. Massage above and below the lips.

Plug In for Balanced Energy

3. Cross Patterning (page 103)

This Cross Patterning technique makes the brain shift between integrated and one-sided hemispheric processing. Use this when it's hard to "do" and "think" at the same time.

1. Do a set of cross march, moving opposite arm and leg to touch together, very deliberately and slowly.

2. Switch to one-sided march (same sided hand and leg move together, like a puppet on a string) also very deliberately and slowly.

3. Alternate sets 6 or 7 times.

4. Always finish on the cross march.

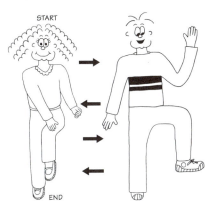

Cross Patterning

4. Cook's Hook Up (page 59)

Position 1: Put your left ankle over the right knee. Grasp your left ankle with your right hand. Place your left hand on the ball of the left foot. Rest your tongue on the roof of your mouth and breathe deeply. When you feel relaxed, move to position 2.

Position 2: Keep your tongue on the roof of your mouth. Uncross your legs. Put your fingertips together gently and breathe deeply. Hold Position 2 for about a minute or two or until you feel calm.

Cook's Hook Up

MORE QUICK SIX

5. Positive Points™ (page 85)

Whenever you feel under pressure, hurt or shocked, take the emotional edge off by holding your "Positive Points." Put your fingertips over your forehead, above your eyebrows. Keep them there while you think through your problem, or talk it out. Holding your Positive Points keeps blood and warmth in your forebrain for better integration.

1. Hold your forehead lightly with your fingertips and tug up slightly.

2. Think through any left over mind chatter, or your stressor.

Now isn't that easy!

Positive Points

6. Be Sense-able

By stimulating these points you are fine tuning yourself for better seeing and hearing.

Eyes: Switch on your eyes by rubbing your "Eye Points." Just above the bony ridge of the occipital protuberance at the back of your head, rub the hollows on both sides to stimulate your visual cortex. (Page 121)

Ears: Give your ears a gentle massage, unrolling your ear edges as well. Notice how this makes sounds brighter, clearer and your attention sharper. You are massaging many acupressure points, stimulating the whole body for a fast pick-me-up! (Page 125)

Eye Points

Rubbing ears

Before we leave this section, quickly turn back to page 32 and repeat the Noticing process thinking of a stressor: Has your personal response already improved? Are you already stepping into self control? Congratulations, and look forward to lots more powerful re-education in the pages ahead! It's important to anchor in improvement by conscious noticing, so the brain truly registers that you now enjoy a higher baseline of integration and functioning.

SECTION 3:

IDENTIFYING THE OBSTACLES

"Stress equals diminished awareness. We humans make the big mistake of believing we're in conscious control simply because we're still conscious. Not so: Under stress we're into knee-jerk duplication of learned re-actions based on negative emotion. Under stress our limitations increase drastically…The worst way to handle stressors is to deny they exist".

Gordon Stokes/Daniel Whiteside, *Tools of the Trade*, p. 58

Section 3:

Identifying the Obstacles

TAKING A CLOSER LOOK AT STRESS

I n our introduction, we had you notice how stress impacts your brain/body state. We also had you experience, via the Quick Six, a taste of how easy self management can be. The next steps toward eliminating your blocks to success and learning, are to give you (1) a more in-depth understanding of what stress is; (2) the inside scoop on its physiological effect; 3) the opportunity to more consciously identify the specific obstacles (external and internal life stressors) that are hampering you; and (4) varied options to start handling them immediately.

What is stress?

The only sure thing in our world is constant change, and *anything* –be it good or bad–that requires the body to spend precious energy adapting is "Stress." Theoretically everything that makes the slightest impression on us, causing us to process new information––from the touch of a child's hand, to a car accident—is a stressor. A wedding or winning the lottery can be as stressful (though more pleasurable) than being fired or divorced. Remember that it is the emotional filter through which we perceive an event that gives the event its label as good, bad or indifferent, and the intensity of its impact.

So stress itself is not the enemy. Actually **sensory stimulation is a "Good Guy"** as it leads to learning and the layering of improved neural (nerve/muscle) connections in the brain and body. Good stress was called Eustress by Dr. Hans Selye, the father of modern stress theory.

The "Bad Guy" is "distress," unresolved stress response, that leads to short circuits in the body's normal electrical communication. Distress is caused by inadequate coping mechanisms in response to the obstacles (stressors) with which we must all deal in daily life.

If you have no stress, you're dead, or floating in a sensory deprivation tank.

All stress goes in one pot, so get rid of the little stressors as well as working on the big ones!

What will be the straw that breaks your camel's back?

A closer look at the pot of stress.

Stress is not simply **emotional** (engaged or divorced, fears, past trauma, new job, other life changes, both positive and negative). It is also **structural** (an accident or falling victim to the "no pain, no gain" syndrome and hurting yourself exercising), **biochemical** (coffee, donuts or pesticides, anyone?), **environmental** (microwaves, fluorescent lighting, toxins etc.), and **behavioral** (inadequate rest, procrastination, perfectionism, etc.).

A little bit stressed is like a little bit pregnant.

There is no such thing as a small stressor. All stressors go into one pot to assault your body's resources. In other words, stress accumulates. It pays to identify and neutralize little, as well as big life issues. Remember, it's almost always a "little" thing that's the last straw, throwing us into dysfunction or symptom.

We invite you to take a closer look at your pot of stress on page 43. Identifying and neutralizing seemingly unrelated areas of stress in your life will improve your overall functioning, guaranteed. However, if you find all this talk about stress *stressful,* feel free to take a break, do the Quick Six activities, and start releasing it now!

A kick in the rear can cause a pain in the head.

We humans are not simply machines; we are mental, emotional, spiritual, as well as biochemical and physical beings. A blow to any of these levels impacts the equilibrium of our whole. When we experience a symptom (imbalance), it has not necessarily been triggered by an obvious stressor (cause and effect). For instance, our back may go out (a structural symptom), not because we lifted a box the wrong way (a structural stressor), but because we had a fight with our spouse (emotional stress) and our back is our weakest link. A person may eat biochemically stressful foods and not understand why he is always prone to emotional depression. Another may be in a car accident and feel lucky to have escaped traumatic physical injury, only to break out in an allergic rash (biochemical symptom).....and so it goes.

All the professional attention in the world won't give us permanent relief from our diverse physical, mental and emotional

Insight: What's in your pot of stress?

Check the boxes which identify the key stressors in your life. What stressors can you remove, reduce, or re-educate?

Emotional
- ❏ Past Emotional Trauma
- ❏ Current & Future Worries & Anxieties
- ❏ Fears & Phobias
- ❏ Lack of Spiritual Awareness/ Religious Faith
- ❏ Fear of Failure and/or Success
- ❏ Past Programming

Chemical
- ❏ Insufficient Water Intake
- ❏ Poor Dietary Choices
- ❏ Nutritional Deficiencies
- ❏ Food and/or Environmental Allergies (sensitivities)
- ❏ Heavy Metal Toxicities
- ❏ Impure Air and Water Supplies
- ❏ Agricultural Sprays
- ❏ Genetic Bio-chemical Defects

STRESS

Physical
- ❏ Musculoskeletal Stress
- ❏ Physical Trauma, e.g. Whiplash
- ❏ Inappropriate Exercise
- ❏ Over-Exercising
- ❏ Poor Posture
- ❏ Maladjustment to Work Place
- ❏ Shallow Breathing

Behavioural
- ❏ Inadequate Sleep and Rest
- ❏ Use (and abuse) of 'Recreational' & Medicinal Drugs
- ❏ Dysfunctional Family Background
- ❏ Perfectionism
- ❏ Procrastination
- ❏ Workaholism
- ❏ Lack of Time Management & Organizational Skills

Environmental
- ❏ Sensitivity to Fluorescent Lighting
- ❏ Sensitivity (allergy) to Specific Colours
- ❏ Sensitivity to Noise
- ❏ Radiation and Electromagnetic Pollution (effects in this area are subtle—often unrecognized and accumulative)

Reprinted from The Top 10 Stress Releasers p. 9

Source: Dr. Wayne Topping

symptoms unless we also identify and relieve the major (often seemingly unrelated) causal stressors. So take a hard look at your "weakest" link—your recurring physical or behavioral symptom. Whatever it is—allergy, depression, sore back, weak stomach, etc., know that it is a combination of all life stressors that has caused you to fall into that symptom. For an improvement that holds, you must ultimately look beyond the straight line cause, to restore balance and well-being to your overall brain/body system.

The continuum of well-being

Think of well-being as a continuum. At 0% you are dead, and at 100% you are brimming with vitality and have a large reservoir of adaptive ability to handle stress. We all fall somewhere on the continuum, with mental, physical and emotional wear and tear starting to show when we fall below 50%. We may wake up in the morning feeling great, but in truth we may be just one sleepless night, two cups of coffee and one unexpected shock away from falling into a mental, physical, or emotional symptom of imbalance.

One little stressor can tip the scales from balance into mental, physical or emotional symptom.

Some theorists believe that this is the aging process: Going below 50% uses up our base, non-replenishable reserves of adaptive energy, until they are exhausted and we die. Therefore, it is believed, genetic inheritance being equal, we can control mental, emotional and physical wear and tear as well as aging, by learning adaptive skills to conserve our stress "shield" and build up our resources. It can be as easy as the activities suggested in this book.

Concentrating on balancing optimal life energy, and moving the individual above and beyond the 50% well-being marker, defines the holistic educational model. In the past, the Western medical treatment model concentrated on treating symptoms when people fell below the 50% mark. Those of us in the complementary health field are deeply gratified by the shift in perception by both the public and the medical profession to recognizing the necessity for personal self responsibility and life style re-education in the promotion of overall well-being. This book forwards that personal re-education.

WHAT HAPPENS WHEN YOU ARE STRESSED?

The Noticing exercise you did on page 32 gave you information on your body's reaction to stress. In order to understand the classic stress response, we have to be aware of its relationship to health and wellbeing. Major learning, health and emotional disorders can be offshoots if stress is not appropriately handled. Remember, the innate fight or flight stress response serves us brilliantly for survival in the moment, such as when we are under physical attack. That is its purpose. We are hardwired to react to threat for our survival (alarm stage), and to resolve that stress, restoring balance to our system (response stage). The stress response does not serve us if we are being asked to consider, but not act upon, a difficult situation.

If we are able to respond actively to a stressor or stressful situation, neutralize it and restore ourselves, there is little long term ill effect. However, we often do not act, because of lack of awareness or coping skills. The stressor remains in our pot of stress, using valuable resources of adaptive energy, leading to what we recognize as the overwhelm stage, where symptoms occur.

So now, let's compare and interpret what you noticed on page 32 to the classic symptoms of the stress response. Just remember, there is no right or wrong, just what showed up for you. Our body is constantly providing an external picture of our internal process.

1. Ohmygawd! a sabre-toothed tiger!

As mentioned, the classic stress response has been wired into our species for our survival. Consider our ancestor coming out of his cave to confront a sabre-toothed tiger. With first shock comes:

Alarm Stage: Blood immediately goes from the front lobes of the brain to the back, "fight or flight" survival centers. This is fitting, as Conan the Caveman had to react instantly and fight or flee for survival—he didn't have time to consider the intellectual options that front-brained activity would provide. Blood also leaves the

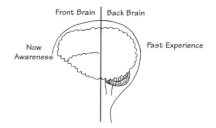

New ideas and choices (a front brain activity) are impossible while we are trapped into back brain, reactive survival patterns.

Stages of the Classic Stress Response

1. Alarm Stage: Blood immediately goes from the front lobes of the brain to the back brain survival centers.

digestive centers and goes to the large skeletal muscles to give him maximum strength. Good idea, since what does digestion matter if you might be dead in a few minutes? We have stories, even today, of petite women picking up cars to rescue a hurt child—a feat impossible without the adrenaline rush that goes along with stress.

Before we return to the adventures of Conan, let's take a moment to use the classic stress response to interpret your own experience. Look back for a moment to your Noticing exercise on page 32. Here are more details of how the body is physiologically reacting to the initial alarm stage of stress.

Did you notice: A change in the way you felt? Did your body begin to sway forward or back, left or right? Swaying can indicate an over focused or underfocused state, as does a feeling of hyper alertness versus spaciness.

Did you notice: Tension or pain in your legs, back, shoulders, neck or jaw? Muscles tense up preparing us for the fight/flight response, so we can fight off the aggressor, or run out of harm's way. However, if we don't respond appropriately, these same tense muscles result in the chronic pain and headache so often associated with stress.

Did you notice: A knot or pain in your stomach or gut? Digestive problems ensue as the blood is diverted from the digestive system and emergency alert orders are sent out by the adrenal system.

Did you notice: A change in your heart rate? Tension in your chest? Were you holding your breath, or breathing more quickly? The brain needs more oxygen under stress, so the heart and lungs start working double time. With shock, we sometimes forget to breathe and get light-headed.

Did you notice: A difference in your vision? Your pupils dilate to increase peripheral vision for heightened awareness of possible attackers. Not so great today if you are stressed because you are studying for an exam, and read everything three times with no focus or comprehension!

Did you notice: A difference in your hearing or comprehension? When we don't feel safe, we don't filter out sound, for fear of missing an

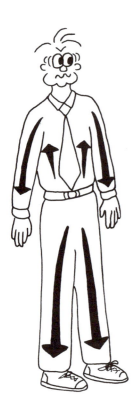

The Alarm Stage: As well as moving from the front brain to the back survival centers of the brain, blood and energy also move from the digestive organs, to the arms and legs for fight or flight.

attack. Concentration and the ability to focus and reason using your higher brain functions is impaired.

Other physiological reactions that impact wellbeing.

Glucose is released, requiring insulin from the pancreas. Over a prolonged period, this may contribute to diabetic conditions. The body releases cholesterol into the blood for energy. The blood clotting mechanism steps up—a great idea if the tiger claws you, so you won't immediately bleed to death. Over the long haul, excessive cholesterol deposits and blood clotting increase the possibility for strokes and heart attacks. Stress hormones created are adrenalin and cortisol. They break down body tissue to provide energy for fight and survival (thus aging us), suppress the immune system, and even decrease learning and memory.[1]

This illustrates how major 20th century diseases and aging itself become offshoots of the stress response which was inbred into our species to serve us brilliantly for survival in the moment. However, we must learn to neutralize the wear and tear of on-going, inappropriate stress reactions by improving our coping mechanisms, allowing us to move into the future in a balanced state.

Now, let's go back and see how Conan is doing.

2. Roast tiger for dinner dear?

Response Stage: If you take action—fight the sabre-toothed tiger—the stress hormones dissipate. So in this instance good old Conan comes out a winner: He immediately acts, kills the tiger, uses up those stress hormones constructively, and brings home meat for supper.

2. Response Stage: If you take action, the stress hormones dissipate.

Humor aside, we shouldn't envy Conan his life style: His survival challenges were unending and correspondingly, his life expectancy was short and not necessarily sweet. His reaction to stress had to be direct, or he would not live to tell the tale. However, in our century, we aren't facing tigers. Stresses today are different, often not allowing for immediate action. More likely it's an unappreciative boss or a difficult family member, and the fight/flight responses are not appropriate. We have little time to deal with the many demands on our system; negative news on TV,

*3. Overwhelm stage:
Energy goes to the
organs of elimination:
liver, lungs, kidney, skin.*

stressful driving, toxic foods, polluted environment, stressful jobs and relationships. While we are trapped into back brain reactive survival patterns, the stress is on-going, and new ideas and choices, a front brain activity, are impossible. Without stress releasing techniques in our lives, such as physical exercise, rest, proper nutrition and the activities in this book, the stress hormones will continue to build until we go into overwhelm.

3. All stressed up and nowhere to go.

Overwhelm Stage is when the symptoms appear that we readily identify as stress. The body realizes you are not going to flee or fight. At this point the body is building up the stress hormones to a dangerous level, and must detoxify. Blood leaves the large skeletal muscles and moves to the organs of detoxification and elimination—the lungs, liver, kidneys and skin. You feel lethargic and have to sit down, going from mild into more serious overwhelm, and may eventually even faint. Fainting (often part of the initial, shocked alarm stage) is actually a brilliant defense mechanism. Fainting is the body's way of getting you out of the picture so you stop generating—and start eliminating—the stress hormones.

Did you notice: Feeling weak, unbalanced or faint? Was it hard to hold up your arms for a minute? Unlocking muscles and weakness are classic signs of neurological confusion and overwhelm.

Instead of cursing our bodies for manifesting symptoms of stress, let us thank them for serving us as best they could for our survival in the moment, and also for giving us an external way of knowing what is happening inside our brain/body. Don't condemn the messenger!

The picture is getting into even clearer focus. We've had you take a close look at the pot of stress in your life, and the non-serving behaviors that have developed as a result . You have experienced how your body physiologically reacts to stress, and understand what this means. Now, let's start tangibly acting upon this insight. The "proactive" process of removing the obstacles starts now!

GETTING OVER THE OBSTACLES

The Three "R"s for managing stress:

1. Remove:

(a) the stressor: Clean up your messy desk (or eliminate any of stressors you've defined in your pot of stress on page 43).

(b) yourself from the stressor: Close the door so you don't have to look at the desk (or change jobs if that's the stressor).

2. Reduce the stressor: Buy some new organizers for your desk (or shuffle your schedule to give yourself more time to tidy up).

3. Re-educate your brain/body response: so your buttons aren't pushed every time you look at the desk, throwing you into overwhelm (or see your messy desk as a sign of a creative mind!).

So let's get going! The next insight activity asks you to pinpoint your first targets in Removing, Reducing and Re-educating your response to stress.

Remove or modify the "small time" stressors that are bugging you. Each one may be little, but in accumulation they become a tremendous load, and use up the adaptive energy you need to cope with the unavoidable major stressors in every life.

Take a look at everything demanding your time and attention. Does it support your life and long term goals? Are you having fun? If not, you are sabotaging and depleting yourself. Take a moment to consider some first steps toward lightening your pot of stress.

Get rid of what you can. Change what you can. Assuming you don't plan to spend the rest of your life running away from the stressors that remain, or choose to manifest illness, you then need to concentrate on #3—Easy tools that re-educate your neurological response to stress.

In the insight activity that follows, identify issues you are immediately willing to address. Then follow through and remove, reduce and/or re-educate them as you progress through the book. The goal is for you to clear out all unnecessary drains on your life energy, and then to consciously take control of your reaction to what remains. The tools in this book will help you to be calm, front brained and coordinated—your best— in all areas of being and doing as you move forward in your life.

Insight: List at least two stressors in each category you are willing to address:

Remove a) the stressor
1.   2.

Remove b) yourself
1.   2.

Reduce the stressor
1.   2.

Re-educate your mental, physiological or emotional response to:
1.   2.

Just one of the thousands of ways to handle stress.

What else can I do?

Naturally there are all the conventional ways of managing stress, such as joining a fitness club, taking a hot bath, meditating, or a thousand and one methods that might work for you. You choose. The only thing you can't choose, is to do nothing!

Our brain/body's desire to attain an emotionally buoyant state has long drawn us to the immediate, synthetic state change triggered by a pill, a drink, a sugar lift or a caffeine jolt. For instance, chocolate contains phenylalanine which triggers release of oxytocin, the same "'bliss, cuddle and bonding" neurotrans-mitter generated when we fall in love, or have a child. No wonder so many of us crave chocolate!

Remember, these external substances mimic our natural "feeling good" biochemicals, bind to our brain's receptors, and depress our body's ability to manufacture our own positive chemical messengers. So barring a medical condition, if we want to help our body attain and maintain a state of emotional, physical and mental wellbeing, it makes sense for us to do all of the following; moderate the stressors in our lives, eat right, sleep right, manage our time, exercise, and do brain/body balancers designed to give our system a chance to naturally manufacture the appropriate biochemicals necessary for a balanced emotional state[2]. The quickest path is to unlock the negative emotional stress response itself, immediately altering brain/body state and chemicalization.

In this book we are concentrating on giving you the tools to re-educate your brain/body reaction to stress in the moment, so that stress doesn't interfere with your ability to remain integrated while learning and doing what you want. Not only can you unlock the hold of stuck stress circuits, but also by preparing yourself with integrating activities from this point forward, you avoid locking in a stress circuit around them in the first place. The buildup of your negative pot of stress can stop right here and now!

NOTES

SECTION 4

RECHARGING YOUR BATTERY

"In the same way that electrical circuits in a house can become overloaded, neurological and physiological signals can become jammed and switch off, blocking the normal flow of brain-body communication. Both Western and Eastern medical authorities recognize the need to keep the electromagnetic circuits of the body...flowing freely."

Paul Dennison, PhD, and Gail Dennison,
Brain Gym Teacher's Edition, page 23

Section 4:

Recharging Your Battery

BALANCING THE BODY ELECTRIC

For years the western world could not explain what made things "alive" and rejected the concept of the body as an energy system because no actual energy vessels (like arteries and veins which carry blood, etc.) could be found upon the dissection table. The Eastern tradition however, has always recognized that basic life systems are "energized." Although still not totally definable, life energy appears to be electromagnetic by nature, and to flow along specific pathways in the body called meridians. Acupuncture and therefore meridian energy, has now become recognized for pain control by Western medicine.

These energy meridians have been mapped out electronically, thermatically and radioactively, using modern technological methods. Current research indicates that meridians contain a free-flowing, colorless, non-cellular liquid which may be partly actuated by the heart.[1] Research is now pointing the way to defining actual structure for these channels.

Meridian energy is actually one continuous, unbroken flow. We work directly with this meridian energy as it nears the surface of the body. Acupuncturists have named these accessible pathways separately, by the life function with which they seem to be associated.

Acupuncturists use needles to work with the meridian system. How fortunate that lay people can benefit by balancing this energy with safe, simple acupressure massage, touch and tracing.

Meridian Trace: Let us take a moment to experience the energy flow of a meridian. Using the palm of your open hand, facing inward, parallel and two inches out from your body, gently run up from below your navel to your lower lip several times. Your palm has enough electromagnetic energy in it to attract and help move the energy up your central meridian, thus enhancing energy flow to the brain and mental functioning. Whenever you

MERIDIAN TRACE:
Stroke up from below your
navel to your lower lip.

need an extra little shot of energy, trace up your central meridian! If you do it slowly several times, you may notice your hand starting to feel tingly, and your head may feel clearer. A downward stroke slows down the meridian energy, so always end on an upward trace, and move your hand to the side, away from the midline, before you let it fall. (Unless you're hyperactive and over-energized: In this case a downward stroke will normalize the excess meridian energy and have a calming effect.)

Electrical messaging: We will explore in later sections how our central nervous system largely relies on electrical polarity-based messaging to carry information from body to brain and back again. To use a simple electrical metaphor, we experience optimal brain/body functioning when meridian energy flow and electrical messaging is balanced and unrestricted, but if our "pot of stress" overloads the normal circuitry, our "fuses" blow. This short-circuiting results in our being either under—or over—energized in different parts of our brain/body system: Either the sparks are flying or the power is down! What's more, this energy pattern can be fused into any of our stuck circuit locks, and reactivated from that time forth whenever we experience similar stressors. In extreme long-term situations, dis-ease can result.

So the first step to releasing the effect of the classic stress response on our performance is to balance the body's electrical and energy systems! We will introduce you to some simple ways to restore energy flow and to improve brain/body electrical messaging. Specialized Kinesiologists use acupressure points, as well as "switches" from other systems (such as the lymphatic and vascular) to effect change on deeper, less accessible levels.

How do we know if our energy system has become compromised? What do we experience when our flow of meridian energy is blocked? First lets do a personal pre-check.

Stress can overload our normal circuitry and blow our "fuses."

Pre-check: Notice your current functioning

❏ Are you aware and alert?

❏ Do you have focus?

❏ Is your concentration and comprehension good?

❏ Does your head feel clear?

❏ Do you feel relaxed?

ACTIVITIES

Drink Water: The #1 Stress Buster & Brain Integrator

Water provides the hydration necessary to conduct the electrical impulses throughout the body, impulses that carry orders from the brain to the muscles and feedback to the brain. Without proper hydration, you'll feel short-circuited and will trigger a stress response, even without other stressors in your life! What's more, pure water is sensed by the brain while still in your mouth via receptors, and instantly corrects the body stress created by dehydration. So sip "instant stress release" throughout the day.

Water is essential for proper lymphatic function, helping to remove waste and toxins from the body. It also allows 1,000-10,000 times more oxygen to bind to the blood, reducing stress on the heart and lungs. An instant brain boost, drinking lots of water heightens energy, improves concentration, mental and physical coordination, and academic skills. It's especially helpful while working with electrical machines (e.g. computers) which can negatively affect our body.

Go with the flow of H$_2$O

Sports doctors suggest a minimum of:

- *One 250 ml glass for every 10 kg of body weight OR one 10 oz glass for every 30 lbs of body weight*
- *Plus: 1 glass for each cup of coffee or caffeinated drink*
- *Plus: 2 glasses for each alcoholic drink*
- *More if you are exercising heavily or under stress*

Keeping these suggestions in mind, experiment and see what amount of water feels best for you.

If you have no medical limitations, doctors suggest one ten-ounce glass per day for every 30 pounds of body weight, and more if one is physically active or under stress. Therefore the average 150 lb. person needs at least five glasses of water per day. Caffeine and alcohol, by the way, are diuretics and you will need an extra glass of water for each cup of coffee you drink and two extra for each alcoholic drink. Raise your glass "to your health!"

"Plug In" For Balanced Energy

"Plugging in" helps to mechanically normalize the energy flow on key meridians, and to minimize the stress response. This simple activity helps you feel more alert, clearer and centered. It can help integrate your left and right brain hemispheres, activate visual centers and strengthen muscles by releasing meridian energy blockages. It's great when your thinking gets fuzzy, or you feel confused.

Make a claw with one hand, and point your five fingertips in a circle around your navel, with your thumb pointing up towards your head. We have strong energy plexuses on the tips of our fingers, and pointing in draws attention to your gravitational center and impacts your meridian energy system. Continue to point inward for the next two steps:

1. For Left/Right Integration—Massage the Kidney 27 acupressure points in the hollows just below the collar bone, on either side of the breast bone—between your first and second ribs. These acupressure points are considered master association points to the entire acupuncture system. Massaging them is believed to affect flow of blood (and oxygen) to the brain.

2. For Up/Down and Front/Back Brain Integration—Massage above and below the lips: You are stimulating the ends of the Central (front) and Governing (back) energy meridians of the body.

This technique was developed by Hap & Elizabeth Barhydt. See their book *Self-Help for Stress & Pain.*

Place the fingertips of one hand around the navel, thumb up. At the same time:

1. Massage under the collarbone, both sides of sternum.

2. Massage above and below the lips.

Cook's Hook Up

This activity enables you to bring all the energy meridians into a more balanced state. Use it any time you are upset, sad or confused. You are linking up front/back, up/down and left/right connections into a figure 8. Electrical energy will begin to flow easily along the pathways, and you may sense increased circulation through your extremities. You are using your own body's electrical forces to normalize energy flow as you deal with thoughts or issues that previously would have blown your circuits.

Begin by sitting in a comfortable chair with your feet flat on the floor.

Position 1

1. Put one ankle over the other knee.

2. Use the opposite arm to grasp the bent leg's ankle.

3. Bend the other arm, and reach over to grasp the ball of the bent leg's foot.

4. Put your tongue on the roof of your mouth and breathe deeply.

Hold this position for a minute or two, or until you feel calm. If you feel like it, reverse the posture. When you feel relaxed, move to Position 2 keeping your tongue on the roof of your mouth.

Position 2

1. Uncross your legs and place your feet flat on the floor, tongue remaining on the roof of your mouth.

2. Put the top of your fingertips together gently and breathe deeply.

As well as being highly energized, the ends of our fingertips have

Position 1

Put one ankle over the other knee. Use the opposite arm to grasp the bent leg's ankle. Bend the other arm, and reach over to grasp the ball of the bent leg's foot. Put your tongue on the roof of your mouth and breathe deeply. If you feel like it, reverse the posture. When you feel relaxed, move to Position 2.

Position 2

Uncross your legs. Keep your tongue on the roof of your mouth. Put your fingertips together gently and breathe deeply.

Hold each position for a minute or two or until you feel calm.

You can do this variation standing up or laying down.

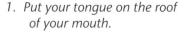

1. *Put your tongue on the roof of your mouth.*

2. *Press one nostril shut and breathe in; release, press the other nostril shut to breathe out. Repeat 3 times.*

3. *Change sides: Breathe in through the nostril previously exhaling, and out through the opposite nostril. Repeat 3 times.*

alternating polarities on opposing hands (thumbs are neutral). When you hold your fingertips together it completes a circuit, and energy flows from the positive to the negative polarity. After a few minutes your fingertips may get rosy and you may feel a throb from moving energy. This is a wonderful posture if you experience cold extremities!

Hold Position 2, thinking of your stressor, for a minute or two or until you sigh, yawn or feel even more relaxed. Cook's Hook Up was developed by Wayne Cook and is especially useful for people who exhibit severe electromagnetic imbalances.

Variation for standing up or lying down—great when you're having trouble getting to sleep

Cross your right wrist over your left wrist and your right ankle over your left ankle (or vice versa). Turn the palms of your hands to face each other and interlace your fingers. Turn your hands in toward your body and up. Put the tip of your tongue on the roof of your mouth, breathe deeply, and when you feel relaxed, move to Position 2, as described above. This variation, called Hook Ups, was developed by Dr. Paul and Gail Dennison for Brain Gym.®

Polarized Breathing

Deep rhythmic breathing has long been recommended for stress control and relaxation (more on that later). Less well known is that our breathing pattern changes from one nostril to the other regularly. This insures an ionization balance, affecting the balance of calcium and potassium in the blood. With stress, the polarization of the cell membrane switches off, and body imbalances begin.

Research has shown that breathing through the nose cools the hypothalamus, which monitors brain chemicals that influence mood. (APA Monitor, Oct. 1990). The breathing cycle is linked to hemispheric dominance in the brain. Right nostril (left hemisphere) dominance correlates to phases of increased activity. Left nostril (right hemisphere) dominance represents rest phases. To change your mood, breathe through your more congested nostril.[3]

It has been clinically demonstrated that the above technique can help balance the brain and body for relaxation and better thinking. Polarized Breathing was first used in Applied Kinesiology by Dr. Sheldon Deal.[4]

Post-check: Body Electric

Do you notice a difference?

❑ Are you more alert?

❑ Do you have better focus?

❑ Is your concentration and comprehension better?

❑ Does your head feel clear?

❑ Are you free of physical signs of stress?

❑ Do you feel more relaxed?

NOTES

SECTION 5:

ve..e..e..e..ry interesting!

COMMUNICATION:
BRAIN TO BODY

"If the brain's organization reflects its experience, and the experience of the traumatized child is fear and stress, then the neurochemical responses to fear and stress become the most powerful architects of the brain."

Sharon Begley "How to Build a Baby's Brain"
Newsweek Special Edition, Spring/Summer 1997, page 31

Section 5:

Communication: Brain to Body

HOW THE BRAIN/BODY COMMUNICATES

N ow that we are better balanced electrically, we can concentrate on some brain/body theory. The first thing you need to do is to give yourself a hand for how brilliantly your body/brain system has functioned up to this moment.

Most of us give ourselves a hard time when we perform poorly under stress. Instead we should be patting ourselves on the back for how well we do function, given the complexity of our human design and considering the amount and kind of environmental, emotional and physical stress with which we have had to cope. It's simply amazing!

We have already discussed what physiological changes you notice when experiencing the classic stress response. Now let's take a closer look at how the brain/body system communicates, to give us an even deeper understanding of how we are affected by the stress response, and to more fully appreciate how we can deal with it on all levels.

Our basic premise is that to be optimally functional, the brain and body must be integrated. Information must be able to flow freely and instantaneously from the body to specific areas of the brain and back again, and from brain part to brain part, each operating separately and as a part of the whole.

The brain/body's most well-known communication system is the nervous system. The brain is the penthouse of the central nervous system, incased in the skull for protection. The rest of the central nervous system is a thin rope of nerve tissue called the spinal cord, which runs down from the base of the brain through the spine. From the spinal cord branch the nerves that make up the peripheral system: 31 fibres from the front carry instructions from the brain to the rest of the body, and another 31 sensory fibers enter

To function optimally, information must be able to flow freely from brain to body.

the rear of the spinal column, carrying information from the body's internal and external sensory detectors, sending it up the spinal cord and into the brain[1]. Another 12 pairs of nerve fibers, called the cranial nerves, originate in the head, and are responsible for everything from taste and smell, to the position of the head and mouth.

Vision is derived from electromagnetic energy; **hearing** and **touch** are derived from mechanical energy; and **taste** and **smell** are derived from chemical energy. All sensory input is converted to electrical nerve impulses which then travel through the neurons,[5] crossing the synaptic gaps via chemical neurotransmitters, ending up in appropriate sorting stations in the brain. Similarly, messages from the brain are encoded in specific frequencies of electromagnetic energy and transmitted to the body, via the superhighway of t**he nervous system**, the **spinal cord**, **motor neurons**, with the help of the chemical **neurotransmitters**, and other chemical networks which we will speak to later. In this way we establish a constant feedback loop with our environment: Sensory information in; motor information out. Our environment informs us, we process and interpret meaning, then we act upon our environment.

We will first explore how the system works from the top down, brain to body. In section 7 we will have a closer look at how communication is occurring in the other direction, body to brain. Finally we will look at the whole picture —a concurrent, miraculous whole brain/body network of communication ongoing simultaneously.

Dividing our brain/body theory into several sections is simply my arbitrary way to chunk down the information into digestible learning modules. Remember, the brain/body is functionally one entity. Contrary to science fiction, where brains in jars can rule the world, our intelligence lives in the whole body, and that is perhaps the most important message of this book.

Theory does give you a deeper understanding of why the processes we use, work. However, knowing the theory is not necessary to get the benefit of the activities, so if you want to get straight to some personal work, you can skip right along to page 81. For the rest of you, who are yearning for learning, here we go!

Contrary to science fiction, where brains in jars can rule the world, our intelligence lives in the whole body.

HOW THE BRAIN WORKS

The brain hasn't changed much for 200,000 years. It's our understanding that's new and improved!

We know that the gross anatomy of the human brain hasn't changed much for 200,000 years, but it's only now with modern imaging devices that we are beginning to understand its biomechanisms. Seventy percent of current knowledge about the brain has been discovered in the last three years, and the intensity of the scientific research assures that our understanding will continue to explode over the next few. It is our intent to give you an easy overview of the brain's role in the stress response. This will hopefully whet your appetite and encourage you to probe deeper into this exciting field of study.

First, for those of you who like your knowledge in a nutshell, we have pulled key brain factoids[2] into a one and a half minute overview, after which we will provide a more detailed look at how your brain communicates.

Brain basics: become an expert in 90 seconds

Your astonishing brain:

- Has too many brain cells to count: estimates project about a trillion, including 100 billion active nerve-cells (neurons) and 900 billion glial cells that cement, feed and protect the active cells.

- Can grow up to 20,000 branches for interconnection and communication on each and every one of those 100 billion neurons. Everything is literally connected to everything. Wow!

- Metaphorically, it functions more like a chemical jungle, with all components enjoying symbiotic relationships, rather than like the old mechanistic image of a computer.

- Works like the worldwide web, relaying individual parts of a message by disparate networks, and reassembling all the pieces at the appropriate brain or body center into an understandable message.

Hi body! Can we talk?

- Is a work in progress: It is constantly reconfiguring its neural highways and reshaping itself chemically and physically as we learn and grow.

- Has a strong emotional component: Attention, focus, long-term memory and therefore learning, are all driven by emotion.

- Metaphorically has three brains in one: an automatic, instinctive (back) brain, an emotional, mediating (mid) brain, and a higher reasoning (cerebral) cortex.

- Has two sides that work in harmony: a detail side (usually the left hemisphere) and a whole picture side (usually the right hemisphere). Excellence in any arena, be it mathematics or art, needs the integration of both hemispheres.

- Sends millions of messages a second, at speeds up to 400 feet per second–200 miles per hour.[3]

- Develops and expresses a multitude of specific intelligences at the same time: We have many ways to be smart.[4]

- Operates on at least four separate wavelengths.[5]

- Is part of an overall transmission system that flashes chemical-electrical messages instantly to every part of your body.

- Is amazingly forgiving and resilient: It makes new connections and adaptations to encourage higher functioning and understanding.

For those of you who have satisfied your need to know and are more interested in the walk than the talk, leave this chapter now and proceed to page 81. For those of you fascinated with the talk as well as the walk, read on for more information!

HOW YOUR BRAIN COMMUNICATES

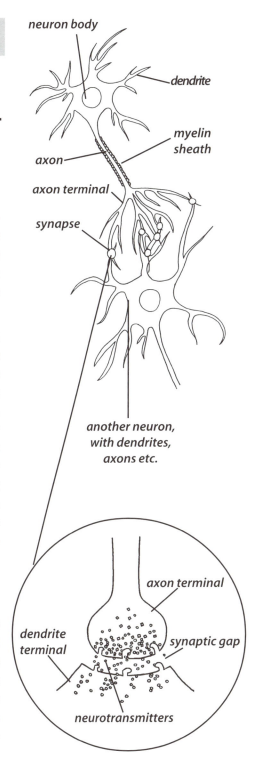

neuron body

dendrite

myelin sheath

axon

axon terminal

synapse

another neuron, with dendrites, axons etc.

axon terminal

dendrite terminal

synaptic gap

neurotransmitters

Meet your relay tag team: your neurons

Like any super highway, traffic is flowing in both directions–sensory and proprioceptive information flowing from the body to the brain, and motor and body function orders going from the brain to the body. Information is sent and received by the brain via nerve cells or neurons (and via informational substances travelling through intercellular spaces—more later!)

At birth, we have a complete set of nerve cells, but only our brain stem is fully functional. As we learn, grow and experience, we develop ever more sophisticated connections between the nerve cells, moving upward toward our higher cortical skills. Each neuron has a large central body with branches called dendrites, reaching out to receive information, and a longer tail-like body called an axon, which transmits information. It's the dendrites which connect a single neuron to a multitude of others by branching outward, waiting to receive information from other axons further up or down the line. The more dendrites a neuron has, and the more neurons it is connected to, the faster the information travels, and the more deeply anchored and sophisticated are the neural networks.

Passing the baton at the synapse

When information (in the form of electromagnetic pulses) reaches the end of an axon, it usually causes the release of chemicals called **neurotransmitters**. These chemicals travel across the tiny space which separates one neuron from another–the synaptic gap. The synapse makes it possible for a single neuron to communicate with a number of neurons simultaneously. Indeed, each neuron may have millions of receptors on its surface. Chemical information gets to the right place because it is received by receptors designed to fit its specific information—like a lock and key.

What's exciting about our brain is that the more we use the system, the more efficient it becomes, with the transfer of information reaching speeds of up to 200 miles per hour. Some researchers claim more! PET (Positron Emission Tomography) scans have shown that the quicker the learner, the more efficient and organized his/her brain activity. Also, efficient neural circuits require less energy. So how do we increase the efficiency of our messaging system? Through learning, practice and using brain/body balancers.

New synaptic connections are made each time we add information or understanding to our repertoire. The speed with which we process that information can also be increased by a process called myelination. Myelination coats appropriate axons with a fatty sheath every time they are used, making them more electrically "leak proof" and efficient.

You didn't drop it this time! Let's practise some more for top efficiency!

As a further aid to efficiency, organization and discrimination, unused brain pathways are actually disabled. Beginning from the first years of life, and particularly around age 11, unused nerve cells are pruned, disrupting synaptic connections. So the old adage "use it or lose it" certainly applies to brain function. Don't panic! We have an abundance of nerve cells from birth, and in the absence of a neurological disorder, we can still function normally even with all the cutbacks.

This is why it's particularly important to expose young children to as many new experiences and varied opportunities for physical and mental development as possible. Ages birth to ten are the years of most dendritic growth: Children are enriching and activating their dendritic association patterns for life. Specialization should come after developing this window of opportunity in early childhood, to increase the basic "hardware" of intelligence. In her research, Dr. Marion Diamond has scientifically proven that the brain grows through environmental enrichment.

In maturity we can still enhance our brain's capacity with new experiences, by doing challenging puzzles, or by mastering new skills with our brain or our body.

THE PARTS THAT MAKE THE WHOLE

You don't need to know what the parts of the brain are in order for you to use your brain effectively. Most of us drive our cars without the slightest interest in the names of the components that comprise the internal combustion engine, while others are passionately interested. The same is true for the brain: If you are one who *is* curious to understand what happens to information within the brain itself, this section is for you! You will find it useful to have a basic understanding of brain physiology. Obviously we are approaching a complex field on a "need-to-know" basis, dealing only with what is necessary to cast light on the model presented in this book.

Current research is pointing toward a modular brain, with tens of millions of different neural networks doing their own little assigned tasks, and intercommunicating throughout the whole brain to create a complex cognitive environment.[6] It is useful as an educational metaphor to categorize the physical brain into three main sections: the back brain, the mid-brain, and the cerebral cortex. As much as we are about to describe the function of different parts of the brain, it's vital to remember that in reality, no part acts alone. Each part must talk to each other part by way of the nerve fibers. Dr. Russell Blaylock expresses it well when he says "No lobe is an island." [7]

The back brain = automatic action

The **back brain** is survival oriented. It handles automatic functions like breathing and heart rate, it's the fastest acting part of the brain, has no sense of time, and will dominate the whole brain when its needs aren't met. In terms of the classic stress response, here's where the Alarm Stage of the stress response first sounds off. We will address three key parts of the back brain.[8]

The **brain stem** is responsible for basic life support. It houses our control centers for the digestive, respiratory, and circulatory systems. It is involved in our classic stress "fight or flight" response. All sensory data travels up the brain stem to reach:

The **reticular activating system** (or RAS), located at the top of the brain stem, which wakes up the brain to all incoming signals, and filters out nonessential information. It is connected to the vestibular system (inner ear balancing). It also acts as a toggle switch that opens and shuts access to higher cortical reasoning (it has axons reaching into the lower reaches of the cortex), based on whether the midbrain is relaxed. Its function is therefore essential for awareness and learning.

The **cerebellum** is sometimes called the mini-brain, and looks like a stalk of cauliflower attached to the back of the brain stem. It is vital for carrying out skilled, complicated movements, routine motor functions like walking (which we learn to do automatically) and balance. It also carries out many of our survival motor mechanisms.

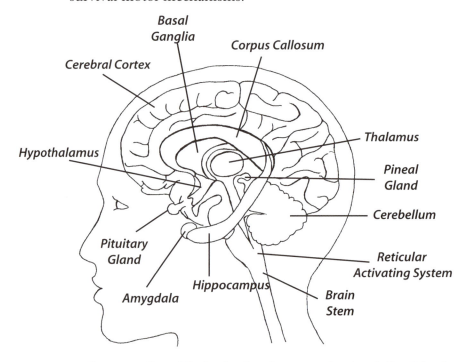

A cross section of the brain, showing approximate relationship of key elements of back brain, mid-brain and cerebral cortex. Several cross sections have been combined into one diagram, therefore are not anatomically exact.

The mid-brain = motivation

Referred to as the Limbic brain in the triune brain model of Dr. Paul McClean, the **mid-brain** is responsible for our biorhythms, body temperature, blood pressure and selection of long-term memory. It has way stations for vision and hearing, and houses the apparatuses that filter our emotions, and determine the intensity of our stress response. A brief introduction to its most important parts: [9]

The **thalamus** monitors and sorts all sensory information (except smell) interpreting pain, temperature and touch. It is the relay center between our sense organs and our higher reasoning cortex, telling our brain what's happening outside the body. From here information filters to:

The **amygdala** which refines the "fight or flight" response, regulates emotion, and is a player in forwarding long term memory. Current brain research is highlighting its role in interpreting emotion which in turn drives attention, learning and memory (more on emotion in section 6).

The **hippocampus,** located next to the amygdala, forms and stores short-term memory, and with the amygdala, converts important short-term experiences (keyed by emotion) into long-term memory.

The **hypothalamus** adjoins the thalamus. It controls body temperature, blood pressure and appetite, waking and sleeping, as well as being a major player in our emotional symphony. It tells our brain what's happening inside our body, and makes necessary adjustments, including the fight or flight stress response, by activating the pituitary gland. The hypothalamus can generate pleasure or anxiety in response to external stimuli. The amygdala regulates those hypothalamic generated emotions, which otherwise would go uncontrolled.

The **pituitary gland** is the master gland of the endocrine system. Activated by the hypothalamus, the pituitary directs the endocrine glands to release hormones that regulate body activity, including the stress hormones activated when we fail to rationally respond to a stressor.

The **pineal gland** acts like a biological time-clock, regulating our day and night cycles. It is activated by light, and controls our growth and development.

The **basal ganglion**, located deep in the brain, connects and orchestrates fine motor function from the cerebral motor cortex, with the gross motor movement from the back brain's cerebellum. It is central to our memory patterns of movement based on thought, including eye patterns and speech.[10] A major gateway to higher cortical reasoning, the basal ganglion is key to intentional, conscious action. As it is stimulated by controlled body movement, our brain/body balancers have a profound impact on it.

A major gateway to higher cortical reasoning, the basal ganglion is key to intentional, conscious action. Since it is stimulated by controlled body movement, our brain/body balancers have a profound impact on it.

Cerebral cortex = reason & insight

The **cerebral cortex** interprets all of our senses, allows us to form complex memory, to reason and solve problems, to interpret sounds, visual images, to acquire language, understand symbols, as well as to analyze information and make decisions. Phew!

The cerebral cortex is made up of two halves (or hemispheres), left and right, joined together by a thick band of nerve cells and connective tissue called the **corpus callosum.** As many of you will know, the right side of the brain controls the left side of the body and vice versa.

The function of these two halves is slightly different. In approximately 97% of the population, left brain functions are described as more logical/linear, and right brain functions are described as more emotional/big picture. (The other 3% have the left/right functions reversed.) In reality, the responsibility for most tasks is shared by both hemispheres, with integrated streams of information crossing the corpus callosum between them.

When information is not flowing readily across the corpus callosum we experience "dis-integration." Under stress we revert to a dominant brain organization profile, and lose the ready input of a big portion of our non-dominant brain and senses. Our ability to think sequentially is cut off from our ability to grasp "the big picture." On the body level, quite literally, the left hand no longer knows what the right hand is doing, and poor coordination can result.

Under stress, communication between the left and right hemispheres breaks down.

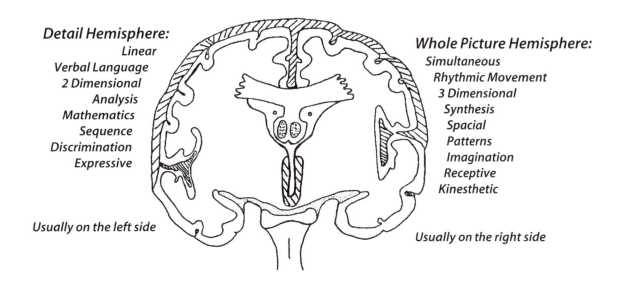

Detail Hemisphere:
Linear
Verbal Language
2 Dimensional
Analysis
Mathematics
Sequence
Discrimination
Expressive

Usually on the left side

Whole Picture Hemisphere:
Simultaneous
Rhythmic Movement
3 Dimensional
Synthesis
Spacial
Patterns
Imagination
Receptive
Kinesthetic

Usually on the right side

*Left/right cross section of the brain, showing attributed functions of
the detail and whole picture hemispheres of the cerebral cortex*

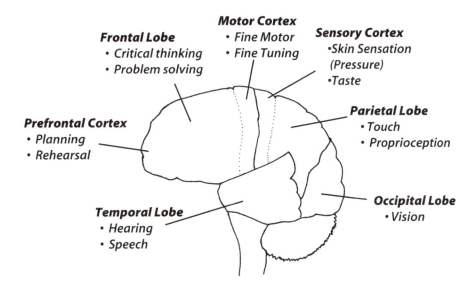

Motor Cortex
• Fine Motor
• Fine Tuning

Frontal Lobe
• Critical thinking
• Problem solving

Sensory Cortex
•Skin Sensation
(Pressure)
•Taste

Prefrontal Cortex
• Planning
• Rehearsal

Parietal Lobe
• Touch
• Proprioception

Temporal Lobe
• Hearing
• Speech

Occipital Lobe
• Vision

*Front/back illustration of the brain showing
attributed functions of the lobes of the cerebral cortex*

Our cortex is also zoned into functional lobes, as seen in the schematic on page 75. Neural communication is zapping between these zones as we make conscious associations between all the senses, movement, speech, and our memory banks. In an unstressed state, the frontal lobe is then responsible for critical thinking and planning. It is the area where we can plan for the future. It is the area of the brain that can be altruistic– it can rise above the classic stress survival responses that would otherwise control our lives, and make choices for a greater good rather than simply personal safety. The frontal lobe is where true choice making lives, and is the key to a whole-brained response.[11]

The whole <u>is</u> truly greater than the sum of its parts: a whole brain/body model for brain function[12]

Dr. Paul Dennison, founder of Educational Kinesiology, and Gail Dennison, speak of brain function in terms of three brain-postural dimensions: focus, centering and laterality. The Dennisons' Brain Gym® movements were designed to integrate all areas of brain function in order to enhance learning.

The focus dimension: "where am I?"

The focus dimension is key for comprehension. According to the Dennisons, we must develop neural connections to determine where we are in space, before we can determine where we "end," and the rest of the world "begins." Movement in space gives us that experiential knowledge. When the front lobes of the cerebral cortex are in balance with the back brain, we gain comprehension with maturity, and, ultimately, achieve focus.

Developmentally, we are dealing with (1) vestibular (inner ear) balance, (2) muscle proprioception (the feedback loop between brain and muscles), and (3) vision. It is my understanding that attention deficit issues are not primarily a product of the higher reasoning cortex, but rather lie with the brain stem and the reticular activating system allowing the flow to the cortex of the non vigilant, filtered communication needed for focus. Babies lay down these developmental connections through movement in a safe environment, movement at first random, then ultimately intentional.[13] In most cases focal ability pre-requires the very

FOCUS DIMENSION
FRONT/BACK
"WHERE AM I?"

Comprehension
BRAIN STEM
lengthening activities

To pre-check the focus dimension:
Have someone gently push you forward with a pressure on your back, then backward with a gentle pressure on the front of your shoulders. Notice if you feel firmly grounded.

movement and vestibular stimulation that is cut off when a child is expected to sit still for the learning process. This ability to co-ordinate the information flow between the back and front parts of the brain is necessary to understanding new information in the context of all previous experience and to being able to act appropriately on the details of a situation. This is the focus dimension. It directly responds to releasing the classic stress response of which the Tendon Guard Reflex is a part. (See page 106)

To activate these parts of the brain: Stand up and sway forward and back. You are activating your vestibular balance system, muscle proprioception and vision, to control where you are in space.

Support for the focus dimension: Lengthening and relaxing activities such as the Rocker™, page 106; the Energizer™, page 107; Leg muscle release page 107, the Owl™, page 126; any other activities that release the tendon guard reflex back & neck muscles.

The centering dimension: "where is it?"

The **centering dimension** is key for the ability to co-ordinate the top and bottom parts of the brain (cerebral cortex to bottom of midbrain), and is essential for our ability to feel and express emotion, to be grounded and well-organized. In order to get ideas from the cortex into action with the brain stem, you need to be balanced with motivation coming from the limbic (midbrain) system. When we are centered, we have a fixed point in our own brain/body to know where we are in space and where things are. This is key to our sense of in and out, and up and down.

To activate this part of the brain: Stand up, then crouch down, up and down. Step forward (in) and step back (out.) Forward and back.

Support for the centering dimension: Balancers include stress management and energy activities such as all the electromagnetic balancers on pages 57 -60, and the emotional balancers on pages 85-88.

Once we know where we are in space, we can judge our relationship to the world around us. Only then can we fully access our higher cortical reasoning skills, or the **laterality dimension**.

CENTERING DIMENSION
UP/DOWN
"WHERE IS IT?"

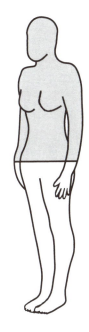

Organization
LIMBIC-MIDBRAIN
Electromagnetic &
Emotional Balancers

To pre-check the centering dimension:
Stand with knees slightly bent, and have someone gently push down on your shoulders, to see if you can remain erect.

LATERALITY DIMENSION
RIGHT/LEFT
"WHAT IS IT?"

Communication
CORTEX
Midline Movements

***To pre-check the laterality
dimension:***
*Have someone exert a gentle
pressure first to one side, then
the other, to see if you can
remain firmly upright.*

The laterality dimension: "what is it?"

Laterality is the ability to coordinate one side of the brain with the other and is fundamental to our ability to read, write, and communicate. This dimension of experience correlates to the left/right integration of our cerebral cortex.

The laterality dimension is key to labelling things and making distinctions. We can ask and answer the question, "What is it?" We master rational cause and effect consequences. We have communication across the midfield, and can move and think at the same time. Flowing freely through the corpus callosum, sensory information is shared appropriately by the two brain hemispheres.

To activate this part of the brain: Sway from side to side, or do a cross lateral movement. (See cross patterning page 103)

Support for the laterality dimension in this book: Cross lateral movements such as Cross Patterning, page 103; Lazy 8s for the Eyes™ page 120; Alphabet 8s™, page 133; The Rocker, page 106; Gait points, page 105; any activity furthering cooperation and coordination across the midline of the body.

What difference does this make to me?

All this information points to the fact that a mixture of integrating activities is necessary if you desire excellence in higher reasoning skills and optimum communication within the brain. With a balance of activities, you are mechanically shifting energy from the brain's survival centers to the whole brain. When you satisfy the needs of the whole brain, you are less at risk of having events dictate your functioning level, and can achieve full focus, comprehension, creativity and the ability to act.

Those of us in the field of enhancing learning and performance are fascinated and grateful to the new scientific findings, as they better explain why the techniques we utilize work. Most simply put, our techniques are brain compatible and they work to integrate the whole brain. Remember to use the brain/body balancers suggested in this book to support and enhance your functioning everyday.

SECTION 6

EMOTIONAL BALANCERS

"It makes no difference to the brain/body whether something actually happened or not. What we feel about experience creates our "reality," our model of the world. Emotion releases hormonal patterns which activate circulation, muscles and organic response as well as etching memory. Again, the brain and body respond in exactly the same way to both real or imagined experience."

Gordon Stokes and Daniel Whiteside, *Tools of the Trade,* page 69

SECTION 6:

EMOTIONAL BALANCERS

IT'S NOT "ALL IN YOUR HEAD"!

Human emotion and behavior are deeply rooted in biology. Researchers such as Antonio Damasio and Joseph LeDoux are determining that emotions provide the bottom line for rational decision-making in our lives, based on survival or social risk. Emotions are felt as bodily states, and are the means through which the mind senses how the body feels.[1]

Emotions then, are apparently evolutionarily developed as a response to the environment to help us survive. The simplistic stand of this book: Control the stress response, control the emotion!

A quick and coy definition which supports the energy model in this book:

E-Motion equals Energy in Motion.

Stuck Emotion equals Stuck Energy.

Indeed, the word emotion comes from the Latin "emovere," which means to agitate and to excite. This is appropriate, since most of our emotions are associated with some kind of instinctive physical response or movement. We laugh, we cry, we tremble, we frown, we fight, we run. Research suggests emotions are a combination of three main parts: (1) An inner experience or feeling, (2) outward behavioral reactions or actions, and (3) physiological reactions.[2] We have already had a first hand experience of all three components in our Insight and Noticing activities thus far. We now know that a change to any of these three fused factors, irrevocably ripples down to the other two. Change the emotion, expect a change in the physiological and behavioural states. Change the behavior, and the emotional and physiological state shifts. Re-educating your physiological state has the power to change your emotional and behavioral states.

"I get emotionally upset thinking about being emotionally upset."

The human system is a chemical factory and much of what makes us who we are is a result of the biochemical information substances which run the checks and balances of our system. Researchers have found the biological messengers of violence, aggression, love and bonding in these neurotransmitters and hormones. They in turn are affected by nutrition, genetics, our relationship with our environment, our state of being, and our conscious choice. The important message of self responsibility is that we are not the helpless products of that chemical messaging: We can consciously shape it.

Current research is shaking up our concepts of the nature of emotion and where it lives, expanding it to a cellular level throughout the body. On page 94 we will talk more about chemical messengers: Of great interest is the work of Neuroscientist Candace Pert, discoverer of the opiate receptor, who speaks to neuropeptides which travel in a secondary free floating nervous system like the endocrine system, as "The Molecules of Emotion"[3]. Antonio Domasio expresses it even more simply: In addition to the "neural" trip of our emotional state back to the brain, our body also uses a parallel "chemical trip".[4] One thing is sure. The emotional "brain" is no longer confined to the classic locations of the midbrain—the amygdala, hippocampus, and hypothalamus —even though these are some of the brain parts dedicated to interpreting and processing that emotion. According to Pert, there are other hot spots throughout the body, particularly where the five senses enter the nervous system.

The midbrain however, is still key to our emotional interpretation and response. Current research suggests that the amygdala decides if information goes to our cerebral cortex for higher rational consideration, or under emotional stress, goes immediately to the cerebellum instead for instant automatic action.

Further, research suggests that the amygdala also determines, based on emotion, what gets layered into long term memory via the hippocampus, and it moderates the hypothalamus which, as described by Robert Sylwester, can activate the fight or

Negative emotion and stress blocks the "flow state" for learning.

flight stress response through its pituitary gland contacts with the endocrine system.[5]

Emotion then, determines whether we are reactive or front brained and reasoned in our lives. As already mentioned, emotion, according to Sylwester, drives attention which drives learning. Emotion is not simply a determiner of how we feel, but of how we live and function.

Section 3 explored the complex array of physical and psychological reactions set off by the stress response. The first line of defense was to get our electrical signalling system up and running smoothly. The next step is to make sure that we are not triggering the classic stress response which triggers off those chemical and electrical impulses underlying our basic animal survival patterns and negative emotions.

What we need now are techniques that allow us to re-educate our body's neural response to emotional stress—that allow us to think of the things, people or situations which previously pushed all our buttons, in a new calm way. We need methods to unhook the emotional triggers that keep us chained to our past experiences. We need to prepare our system for successful outcomes with mental rehearsal, pre-establishing neural pathways for success. Bottom line, we need a way to assure energy remains in the frontal lobe of the cerebral cortex, where clear insight is possible, the future can be evaluated and planned with fresh options in the light of what the back brain already knows. It sounds like it should be complicated, but nothing could be easier. No additional tools are required. You are holding everything you need in the palms of your hands.

Mental Rehearsal:
As far as the brain is concerned, when you visualize a successful outcome in detail, you are establishing the experiential connections to achieve your goal.

This house has many doors

There are many complementary approaches for dealing with emotional distress, some psychological, some physiological, some behavioral, some nutritional. All claim to be effective methods. Indeed they may be! There are many doors into the same house, and the house of which we speak is "balanced energy."

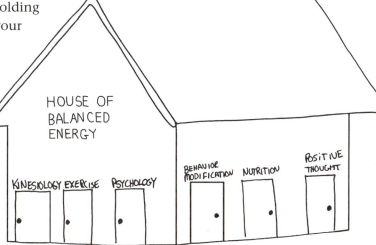

As we have explored, our emotional experience consists of a feeling, a physiological and a behavioral response. Change any of these three parts and the whole circuit lock is broken; the emotional experience is transmuted.

Remember the techniques here are beneficial for handling your emotional stress response in the moment. For deep seated blocks, a re-triggering of the non-serving response and a need to repeat the balancing activities is not unusual. For permanent and long term handling of these deeply etched patterns, repetition and/or a more involved process may be necessary.

One of the strengths of my field of Specialized Kinesiology is that it honors and incorporates processes from many modalities within a framework of self education via biofeedback. I invite you to more deeply explore some options in this field.[6] I also encourage you to explore other mind/body disciplines and therapies.[7]

Now lets get back to work with our emotional pre-check.

Pre-check: Emotional Stress

Think of a stressful situation you must deal with. Do the Noticing process on page 32, and note your reactions to your stress. Note your brain/body's reactions:

Mental:

Physical:

Emotional:

It's not all in your head!

ACTIVITIES

NOT TO WORRY! HOLD YOUR POSITIVE POINTS™!

Whenever you feel under pressure, hurt or shocked, take the emotional edge off by holding your Emotional Stress Release Points, also called Positive Points in Brain Gym. Emotional Stress Release was first presented in Touch For Health in the early 70's, and involves holding the neurovascular holding points that balance both the Central (mental) and Stomach (digestive) energy meridians.

1. Put your fingertips gently on your forehead, above your eyebrows.

2. Tug up slightly on the skin, while you think through your problem, pre-rehearse a successful outcome, or talk it out.

The energy in your hands is enough to keep blood and warmth in your front brain, and stops the classic stress response (flow of blood from front brain to back survival centers) right in its tracks. Now you can perceive new ideas, and make creative choices in the light of what you already know, even when you're stressed.

Combining Mental Rehearsal with Positive Points creates a rocket trajectory to excellence. Mental rehearsal has already been proven effective by athletes, sports coaches, educators and psychologists. As already mentioned, new brain research supports the idea that what we imagine is as real to our brain as what we have actually experienced. Thinking fires off the same circuits as doing. Adding Positive Points to mental rehearsal assures we are programming our imagined action in as a whole-brained, integrated activity, with full power in the frontal lobes!

POSITIVE POINTS™

1. *Hold your forehead lightly, pulling up lightly on the skin.*

2. *Think through your problem, the front-brained way*

   Now that's easy!

Stress releasing the past:

This technique can be used to defuse the stuck circuit lock triggered by any stressful memory or fear. All you need do is to hold your Positive Points while you remember the incident, until you notice yourself feeling more relaxed. Next, reframe the outcome by imagining as many changes as possible to the old stressful memory, and visualizing a positive outcome with as much sensory detail as possible to create the new "reality" you deserve. Make it up, if you have to! You hopefully break the hold of the old memory, by adding in new information. De-fuse the bad, so you can keep front brained when you think of it, and infuse the good, to lay down positive neural "memory" traces.

Stress releasing the future:

Hold your Positive Points while you visualize an upcoming challenge—a presentation, an exam, an interview, a race (any situation where you want to be calm and focused)—from beginning to end. Anticipate everything that could happen, good or bad. See yourself handling all possibilities with coolness and grace. See your successful completion with as much sensory detail as possible. Awareness of colors, sounds, smells, tastes and body sensations which occur while holding your Positive Points activate more areas of the brain which could be tied into a circuit lock.

Other variations:

For powerful emotional stress management you can also have someone hold your Positive Points while you do Cook's Hook Up. The limb link ups of Cook's Hook Up balances all the meridian energy in the body: back/front, up/down, left/right. Holding Positive Points makes sure energy stays in the front cerebral cortex for better thinking and creative problem solving.

Another variation, called Frontal/Occipital Holding, is to lightly hold your forehead with one hand and hold your other hand over your visual cortex at the back turn of the skull. This draws energy and warmth also to the primary visual cortex, the area of the brain that must "see" clearly what really happened or visualize the best future action if you are to make successful choices and plans (a front brain activity). This variation is from *Three in One Concepts*.

Combine Emotional Stress Release with Cook's Hook Up for powerful stress management!

Other applications:

Pain relief: For minor bumps and ouches, hold pain spot with one hand, and forehead with the other. Great for soothing children.

If you are under pressure on a test, rest your forehead on one hand while you write with the other.

Always remember to notice the improvements in how you feel physically and mentally after the process, to help anchor in your brain/body's new improved functioning.

Taking Emotional Stress Release a Step Deeper with Eye Rotations

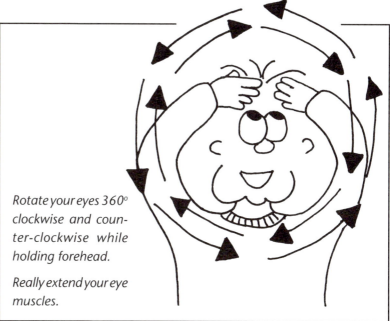

Combining Eye Rotations with Positive Points gives you a powerful tool to control your emotional well being.

Couple the holding of your "Positive Points" with eye rotations for an almost instant emotional quick shift. This efficiently accesses the whole brain for stress release.

Bits of memory (color, smell, sound, taste, etc.) are embedded throughout the brain. Our eye direction shifts each time we access a different part of the brain. Neuro-Linguistic Programming (NLP) studies in depth how to determine the precise eye direction needed to access a particular memory or function. A short cut was developed by Dr. Wayne Topping, who determined that all we need do is a full eye rotation, which will activate *all* areas of the brain at once. Take care to extend your eye muscles in all directions.

Rotate your eyes 360° clockwise and counter-clockwise while holding forehead.

Really extend your eye muscles.

1. Hold your Positive Points. Slowly and carefully rotate your eyes clockwise and counter-clockwise at least once. Overlap when changing directions. Really extend your eye muscles. Repeat until the eyes rotate smoothly. If you trigger an emotion, feel an eye jerk or pain in any one direction, continue looking in that direction while holding your forehead until the stress reaction eases.

Think of a positive situation. Anchor positive energy into cellular memory on your body, for later reactivation.

2. Program in a quick dose of positive emotion whenever the need arises. Say "I Feel _____(emotion or state of being)" while holding your forehead and rotating your eyes. This puts the affirmation directly into the subconscious, and efficiently accesses the whole brain for deep stress release. For example, after narrowly avoiding a car crash, heart pounding, I got to the side of the road and did eye rotations on "I feel calm" and "I feel safe." I was suffused with those feelings, and within two minutes, my stress reaction dissipated and I was able to proceed on my way.

Anchoring Yourself in Calm Waters

Prepare yourself for stormy seas by providing yourself with a safe harbor you take along with you! Anchoring takes advantage of the fact that we lock emotion into the body's cellular memory when experiencing both real and imagined situations. By locking into our body circuits a positive safe place or happy experience, we can quickly infuse any deteriorating situation with a boost of good positive energy, thus breaking the reactive circuit lock triggered by the stressful situation.

1. Decide on an inconspicuous trigger point you can press in public without calling attention to yourself. e.g. Press into your thigh or the palm of your hand.

2. Think of your favorite place or happiest time. Vividly recreate it in your mind. See it. Smell it. Hear it. Touch it. Taste it.

3. Firmly push on your anchor point to lock your positive feelings into a physical circuit.

4. When you are under stress and starting to "lose it," press on your anchor point to be flooded with positive energy to counteract your stress, and to avert the negative reactive circuit lock.

This technique was originally derived from Neuro Linguistic Programming (NLP), and is an ideal one to use for job interviews and definitely great for calm parenting!

Post-check: Emotional Stress

Think of your stressful situation again. Redo the Noticing process on page 32, and note the improvement in your body reaction as you visualize your emotionally stressful situation. Is there a difference in how you feel:

Mentally:

Physically:

Emotionally:

Most people report that their stressful situation no longer feels like such a big deal, and their bodies have been relieved of stress related physiological reactions.

What differences have you noted? Is there any area where you desire further improvement?

NOTES

SECTION 7

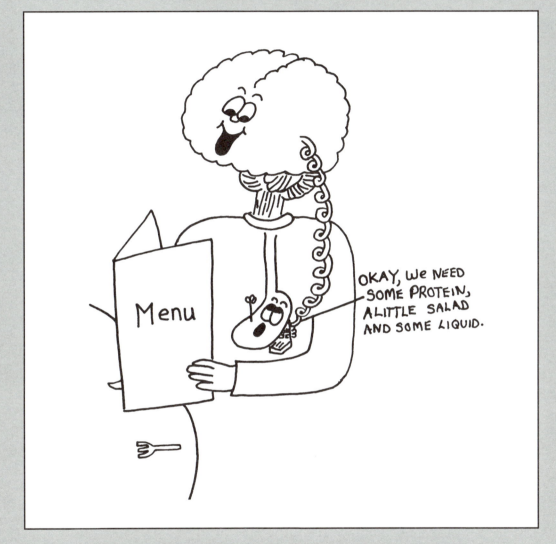

COMMUNICATION: BODY TO BRAIN

"Our emotions affect our structure; our structure affects our emotions. When we change one, we change the other. If we are excited, our posture reflects it, and if we are depressed our posture demonstrates that. Our chronic, usual emotions which dominate us are correlated with our structure. It is now known that certain chemicals manufactured in the brain and other organs may affect the emotions, senses and thinking. The reverse is also true: how we feel, sense and think also affects our body chemistry and causes the manufacture of chemicals within us. When we change our emotions the chemistry of our bodies changes."

Dr. John Thie, "The Pyramid of Touch For Health",
***Touch For Health International Journal,* 1987, p.6**

Section 7:

Communication: Body to Brain

HOW THE BODY COMMUNICATES

We've introduced you to the brain-to-body component of the communication loop, and to our nervous system. This chapter deals with that other side of the moebus strip—a closer look at the simultaneously flowing body-to-brain communication network. Remember, our intent is to introduce you to concepts that support the re-education of our brain/body system for better communication—not to turn this book into a graduate course in anatomy, biology, neurology, immunology, psychology, or for that matter, philosophy. Our bibliography refers you to some wonderful books that will give you scientific, anatomical detail of how the individual body systems work.

Hey we're supposed to be keeping the connections flowing here! WAKE UP and get moving!

From the outside in: body language

Our body is an external mirroring of our internal state. Called "body language" by some, we can intuitively tell how colleagues are feeling by the positioning of their bodies, the look in their eyes, their gestures and facial expressions. By the same token, by deliberately assuming the body posture of a particular state, we can shift our emotional state. Try this experiment:

Stand up. Slouch your body in a depressed stance, drooping despondently toward the floor. Let your face and voice almost weep, as you say in a depressed tone " I've never been so happy in all my life! I feel like dancing!" It feels ridiculous, doesn't it? Almost impossible to say, without starting to smile.

Now stand up tall. Put up your arms in a classic victory "YES!" posture. Smile and say with enthusiasm "I am so depressed, life is not worth living!" Once again, it feels ridiculous to say that in a positive posture.

Now, once again assuming your positive victory posture, cheer: "Life is great! Yes!" Feel the invigoration and the rightness of combining positive thought with positive body stance, movement and energetic sound.

Research has shown that body posture alters the temperature of the brain, which in turn alters speed of chemical body reaction, emotion and outlook. A sample experiment referred to in *The Brain Pack* had subjects rate cartoons for funniness while holding a pen in either their teeth or their lips. Holding a pen in the teeth forced their faces to smile. Holding it in their lips forced them to frown. Those with pens in their teeth, forcing a smile, found the cartoons funniest.[1]

Meet your chemical messengers

Researchers are coming to believe that only a small percent of neuronal communication actually occurs at the synaptic gap between neurons. In her book, *Molecules of Emotion,* Candace Pert gives a clear account of this new paradigm of body/brain communication. Informational substances—a term coined by the late Francis Schmitt of MIT to describe a variety of messenger molecules (neurotransmitters, peptides, hormones etc.)—are manufactured in cells throughout the body, not just the brain. Alongside the conventional model of synaptic neuronal circuitry, Schmitt proposed a parasynaptic, or secondary parallel system, where chemical informational substances can sometimes act like neurotransmitters, but are much more likely to travel through extracellular space, in the blood and cerebrospinal fluid[2], looking for their specific receptors in the brain and body organs, communicating and activating far from their point of origin.[3] This is another example of the two-way communication between the brain and the body.[4]

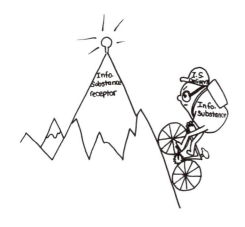

Informational substances can go off the beaten track to find their specific receptors.

In summary, current research suggests all systems—nervous, immune and endocrine—are communicating and reacting to each other, affected by, and affecting emotion. All the messengers are not originating in the brain, rather in many locations in the body.

Repeating what was mentioned in our introduction, body movement definitely enhances the manufacture, balance and transportation of informational substances and flow of subtle energy in our body. Endorphin production is activated by movement, as the famous runner's "high" confirms. Slow lateral movement stimulates the manufacture of dopamine[5] in the frontal lobe (affecting our ability to see patterns and learn faster), the limbic area (controlling our emotions), and the basal ganglion (intentional movement) of the brain.

Our motor system

The motor cortex is our bridge into the higher reasoning frontal lobe. One of the first parts of the brain stimulated by gross body movement is the basal ganglia. Robert Sylwester, in his book *A Celebration of Neurons*, speaks to a three-part model for our motor system. First, many parts of our brain, especially the frontal lobes, are involved in the thinking and planning processes that lead to a conscious decision to move. Second, our conscious starting, walking and stopping actions are processed principally in the basal ganglia, where the conscious intent is activated into movement. Third, our cerebellum at the lower back of our brain takes over the routine walking actions, etc., as soon as consciously begun. Our basal ganglia (along with other brain areas) will monitor the trip, and resume conscious control when required to navigate new obstacles.[6] We shift between automatic, known movement, and conscious intention. But to get started we need the basal ganglia active. Movement comes first, the same way that developmentally a baby moves at first arbitrarily, laying down the neural patterns that become the underpinnings for later sophisticated conscious activation circuits.

Movement of the core gross muscles stimulates the Reticular Activating System—the wake up call to the brain to new sensory information. In many cases of learning disability, there is poor neural development, scar tissue, or a stress response causing incomplete messages to pass through the brain stem and the RAS. Specialized Kinesiologists use specific repatterning processes to encourage the development or restoration of appropriate communication links through the whole brain.

Developmentally, the vestibular (inner ear vibrational balancing system) is key. It is the first system (hearing) to be developed. It is fully myelinated in utero by 5 months, whereas vision doesn't fully develop till 8 months after birth, and full eye teaming doesn't come in until approximately 8 years old. Not to get too philosophical in this book, but the new science seems to be pointing to a vibrational information field which infuses and resonates with the human organism. The inner ear cochlea is designed to

Movement stimulates the production of our body's "feel good" messengers.

pick up this vibration. Our receptor cells throughout the brain and body also vibrate to attract information, and are major players in our communication with the outside world. Anything that stimulates them, helps us: So body movement to activate the vestibular system is beneficial.

Kids instinctively know what's good for them: they're activating the vestibular system by squirming, running and jumping– rebuilding over scar tissue and activating the balance system. Jean Ayres, author of *Sensory Integration and the Child*, emphasizes tactile and vestibular (touch and balance) stimulation for healthy development. Kids labelled Attention Deficit Disorder need lots of vestibular stimulation (as mentioned in our discussion about the Focus Dimension). As we will explore later in more detail, touching is also important, especially on the face and hands where there are lots of nerve nets.

As already expressed in Section 1, Specialized Kinesiologists are dealing with a very simple energy model, where a stuck state of being, manifesting as a mental, physical, or emotional block (or all three) is mirrored in subtle energy and communication imbalances in the body—often a stuck muscle response.

The Motor Cortex is our bridge into the higher reasoning frontal lobe. So if you want to think better, get a move on!

Finally! how a muscle communicates

A clear muscle circuit communicates instantly with the brain, holding strong or relaxing as appropriate. For instance, when you step forward on your right leg, your quadriceps muscle, on the front of your thigh, contracts. The hamstring muscle on the back of your leg, relaxes. On your left leg the reverse is happening: hamstring on, and quadriceps relaxed. As the left leg swings forward into the next step, instantly the orders reverse. This is our walking gait—just one of many automatic circuits built in to let us function painlessly and efficiently without thinking about it.

A stressed circuit either cannot stay on, OR cannot shut off. If the messaging gets confused due to stress or trauma, automatic circuits do not fire appropriately, and we tire or experience pain.

Experience brain/muscle communication

Sit in a chair and raise one leg up with the knee bent, lower leg angled 45°, and hold it firm. It is the quadriceps muscle that is raising your leg. With your hand, push down on the center of the thigh to see if the muscle is "on" (able to resist your pressure). Hopefully it is.

Now sedate (turn off) the muscle by firmly pinching inward in the belly of the muscle, in the up/down direction of the muscle fibres (see drawing below). Pinch, pinch. Now with your hand push down again on the top of your raised quadriceps with the same pressure as before. Did your muscle release?

In the belly of the muscle are tiny proprioceptors called **spindle cells**. Their job is to tell the brain whether a muscle is too contracted or too relaxed. By pinching them closer together, you sent an instantaneous message to the brain, "too close, too close!" and the brain responded with the order to lengthen (relax) the muscle, momentarily turning it off. A normal muscle will reset itself quickly, but experiment with switching the muscle "on" again.

Raise your leg once again, this time tonifying the muscle by using your two hands to pull outward from the center of the belly of the muscle, along the direction of the muscle fibre (see drawing next page). Once more push down with your hand on the top of your thigh, using the same amount of pressure. Was your muscle able to resist your pressure? You pulled the spindle cells wide apart, and they sent the message "too loose, too loose!" Your brain responded by instantly contracting the muscle, turning it strong again.

Congratulations! You have manipulated a muscle and received a functional read-out from the brain and central nervous system––biofeedback via a muscle check.

For those who did not get the expected response, have a drink of water, and repeat the process with a stronger pinch and/or a stronger push. If that still does not get the desired response, know that there could be inappropriate messaging from that muscle to the brain. Not to worry, but if you want to look into it further,

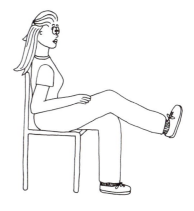

Hold up leg firmly, and push down in the center of your thigh to test for "on" muscle.

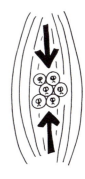

To sedate a muscle: Pinch inward on the belly of the muscle. Spindle cells say "Too tight!", and the brain relaxes the muscle.

To tonify a muscle: Pull outward from the belly of the muscle. Separated spindle cells send the message "too loose," and the brain tonifies the muscle.

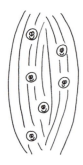

Spindle cells are "just right", until the next time they need to talk to the brain!

contact a trained kinesiologist or health care professional[7], as easeful movement is always a by-product of muscles that have a clear communication with the brain.

Muscle checking as low-tech biofeedback

Specialized Kinesiologists value muscle checking as a superb, simple means of biofeedback. About 95% of information from our body is unconscious, and the muscle check plugs us in to this level, providing a stress/no stress read-out directly from the brain and the central nervous system. Muscles have their own intelligence, and it is profitable to use muscle checking to make sure their intelligence is communicating appropriately to the brain. Muscle checking allows a readout of over and under energy via a muscle indicator. Used appropriately, it is particularly useful in pinpointing and moving through energy circuit blockages to learning.

In the same way you checked on the functioning of your quadriceps muscle, you can check other muscles. This can give you feedback to the support individual muscles (and sensory organs) are giving you in any given task. You can do specific work to re-educate the "rebels," to help you perform better, or to remediate pain. For instance, while spindling the muscles seems such a simple technique, it can have a profound impact, as the following story illustrates.

After a lecture I gave on a cruise ship, having the audience do the same quadriceps demo you just did, a woman came running back in glee. She had left the room, and walked down several flights of stairs before she realized something was different: Her chronic knee pain, for which she had even had surgery, was gone! As a non medical person, all I can assume is that working with the quadriceps the way she did, was enough to clear some gaits circuitry confusion, and this reprogramming changed the way the quadriceps supported her knees. Wouldn't it be wonderful if it were *all* that easy! And who is to say that it is not, until we've opened ourselves to the possibility of simple solutions. A Touch For Health class and/or consulting a licensed health practitioner who manipulates or mobilizes stuck joints can result in a noticeable difference in posture, alignment and performance. In the meantime, the integrating activities in the following section will help you to keep a step ahead!

SECTION 8

BRAIN/BODY BALANCERS

"We develop our neural wiring in direct response to our life experiences. Ability and increased potential grow hand in hand. As we grow, as we move, as we learn, the cells of our nervous systems connect in highly complex patterns of neural pathways. These patterns are organized and reorganized throughout life, allowing us greater ability to receive outside stimuli and perform the myriad jobs of a human life."

Dr. Carla Hannaford, *Smart Moves, Why Learning Is Not All In Your Head*, **page 17**

Section 8:

Brain/Body Balancers

GET MOVING AND MAKE THE CONNECTION

W e may have prepared ourselves to move forward in our lives electrically and emotionally, but is our body going to go along for the ride? Will all our body circuits support us with normal, free flowing movement?

Remember that under stress we manifest all sorts of physiological changes that impact the brain/body and ease of movement. We revert to our dominant brain organization pattern, losing our whole-brain power to make good decisions or to enjoy optimum coordination and performance. Stuck stress circuits put us on auto pilot with conditioned ways of responding that are in-grained and well myelinated, albeit less than desirable. We experience the tendon guard response (tension along the back of the body from the neck all the way to the ankles as we prepare for flight or flight). Our breathing becomes shallow, tension in our jaw persists, and chronic headaches can develop amongst other stress related symptoms.

We might consciously will and intend an integrated, organized whole-bodied response, but it's often necessary to retrain the brain/body to release those old automatic patterns. These next activities will allow us to re-educate our body's communication network, hopefully returning us to optimal functioning, allow-ing us to "do" and "think" at the same time.

Repetition deepens neural integration. Unlike aerobics, where if "you don't use it, you'll lose it", with brain integration tech-niques, the more you do them, laying down improved neural networks, the less you have to do to maintain them. Do the following balancing activities slowly and deliberately. At this time you may want to review page 29 to re-familiarize yourself with the concept of the Information Sandwich, and the function of the pre- and post-check. It's also perfectly fine to just jump directly in and experience the activities without the pre-check.

Is it easy or hard to think and do at the same time?

Remember the information sandwich to first identify areas to improve, and then to anchor in that improvement.

Pre-check: Brain/Body

❏ **Think of an activity for which you desire better brain/body functioning** (eg. better tennis game).

❏ **Roleplay the action using your whole body** (i.e. Act out your tennis swing.) Then march in place, opposite arm and leg moving (see next page to understand what this activates)

❏ **Do the noticing activities** you have learned up to this point (particularly page 32). Jot down how your body acts and reacts.

If your quadriceps muscle responded appropriately for you in the spindle cell exercise on page 97, you can choose to use the same process again to get a muscle check read-out regarding any stressful situation requiring your body's coordination.

Check off "holds" or "relaxes." If any of these checks are different from your previous experience , this means that neurological confusion in your muscles has occurred because of stress associated with your challenge.

❏ **Think of and roleplay your activity once again. Quickly sit down, and do a muscle check on your quadriceps:**

1. Lift your leg and lightly resist while pushing down on thigh. Your leg should be able to hold. ❏ Holds   ❏ Relaxes

2. Pinch in belly of muscle, and push down on thigh again. Muscle should relax. ❏ Holds   ❏ Relaxes

3. Pull apart in belly of muscle and muscle check again. Muscle should be strong once more. ❏ Holds   ❏ Relaxes

❏ **Note differences:** ❏ Wouldn't hold strong when appropriate
                                           ❏ Wouldn't relax when appropriate

❏ **A co-ordination check:** Grasp your nose with your left hand, and reach across your face with your right arm to grasp your left ear. Now switch —left hand grasps right ear, and right hand grasps nose. Switch again. And again. Does it confuse you? Is it easy or hard to think and do at the same time?

How is your co-ordination? Grasp opposite ear and nose, then switch quickly.

ACTIVITIES

Cross Patterning: A Jump Start to Brain/Body Integration

This Cross Patterning technique from *One Brain* is simple to learn and activates (in some cases re-establishes) communication between the two brain hemispheres and the whole body. It works by stimulating the brain to shift between integrated (both sides) processing, using a cross lateral (two-sided) march, and parallel (one-sided) processing using a uni-lateral (one sided) march. Use it whenever it's hard to "do" and "think" at the same time.

Each brain hemisphere controls the opposite side of the body. So by intentionally moving an opposite arm and leg across the midfield, we fire off both brain hemispheres at the same time, creating and myelinating better neural connections over the corpus callosum. This cross lateral movement stimulates the whole brain—the vestibular (balance) system, the reticular activating system (the brain's wake-up call!), the cerebellum (automatic movement), the basal ganglion (intentional movement), the limbic system (emotional balance), and the frontal lobes (reasoning). As already mentioned, slow cross lateral movement also increases dopamine levels in the brain (enhancing our ability to see patterns and to learn faster).

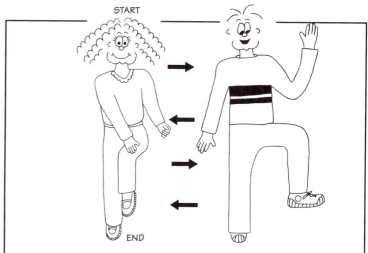

START

END

1. Do a set of cross march, moving opposite arm and leg together.
2. Switch to a set of one-sided march (same hand and leg move together).
3. Alternate sets 6 or 7 times.
4. Always finish on cross march.

When we then switch to a same side arm and leg movement, we deepen the neural netting that assures our ability to quickly shift with ease and full access, to each individual hemisphere as needed. The intent is never to be "stuck" in any one pattern of brain communication. Multiple connections and instant flexibility are the key!

If you are physically challenged, you may do this technique sitting or lying down, using small arm and leg movements.

1. We start off with a cross march (commonly called cross crawl), slowly and deliberately crossing the right arm over the midline of the body to touch the opposite raised leg (left thigh). We then release that arm and leg, and deliberately lift the opposite (left) arm to touch the right thigh. Do 6 or 7 pairs (one set) of the cross march with deliberate, controlled movements and relaxed shoulders. Notice if it is automatic and easy, or if it requires deliberate thought and effort.

2. Switch over to a one-sided march. In a controlled manner raise the same side hand and leg together, then lower them. Now raise the other side's arm and leg together, and lower. Imagine being a puppet on a string. Do 6 or 7 pairs (one set). This fires off one side of the brain at a time. Notice how it feels. Does it require conscious intent, or is it effortless?

3. Alternate between a set of cross marching and a set of one-sided marching, 6 or 7 times or until the shift is smooth. *Always* end on cross march. Our goal is to automatically do the cross march (this means that if you aren't thinking about it, you will cross over the midline), yet to be able to stop and intentionally switch to the one sided march with ease—a necessary step for the processing of new information.

Many variations (e.g. touching your opposite heel behind your back) can be used to keep cross marching fun and fresh, and fast music can be used for variety after the process becomes automatic.

Some people find it is stressful to use both sides of the brain and body at the same time. This is usually due to the stress response putting us into a specific Dominant Brain Organization pattern regarding a particular challenge.

If you experience difficulty with this activity it is a sure sign that you stand to benefit greatly from our brain/body activities and the resulting better neural connections over the corpus callosum. A session with a Specialized Kinesiologist for more profound repatterning procedures could prove extremely beneficial.

Cross Patterning can be used to aid memorization of data. It can also be used as an integrating "clean sweep." While alternating

If you are physically challenged, you may do this technique sitting or lying down, using small arm and leg movements.

between the cross march and the one-sided march, think of any stressful situation (a presentation, sales call, examination, meeting, etc.), then use positive affirmations to further aid stress management. For some sample affirmations, see page 149.

Gait Points

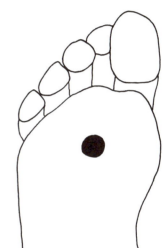

Here's a wonderful way to start your day! Stimulating gait switches will help coordinate body movement and balance. They are the mechanism that co-ordinates the natural opposite arm and leg movement that I referred to in Cross Marching. This most frequently used gait reflex is involved in making sure that as we move our left leg forward we bring our right arm with it, and that the right leg and left arm go back at the same time. Similarly, we have side gaits and back gaits, responsible for our coordination and grace as we step sideways or backwards. Gait points also stimulate meridian energy circuits that feed into the brain.

It's easy to activate the Gait Points:

1. Firmly massage the points on the top of your feet, just above the webbing of the toes, between the metatarsal bones. (These would be the knuckles of your feet, if feet had knuckles.) These points can be very tender the first few times you rub them. Just massage lightly, increasing pressure until the "ouch" abates.

2. Continue massaging the points on the sides and bottoms of your feet.

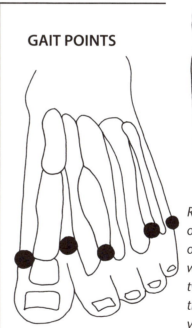

GAIT POINTS

Rub firmly for 15-20 seconds: the points on the top of your feet just above the webbing of the toes, between the bones, and on the bottoms and sides of your feet as shown.

Remember, you are stimulating a number of essential reflex points, and integrating your brain/body for walking, moving, sports and learning—definitely putting your best foot forward! The gait points activity is from *Touch for Health* by Dr. John Thie.

Speaking of best foot forward, give your feet a good massage to stimulate your proprioception for balance and gravity. An easy way to do this is to place a tennis ball under one foot while standing on the other foot and rolling it about. Change feet and repeat.

Releasing The Tendon Guard Reflex

Part of the classic stress response is the tensing of the muscles on the back of our body, from the Achilles tendon in the ankle to the top of the spine and head, for fight or flight. It can cause loss of flexibility. The tension can be released by activities to lengthen our leg, shoulder, spine, abdomen and back muscles. Freeing the tendon guard reflex balances our brain and impacts our mental and emotional stress responses. Spinal flexibility as a metaphor represents one's ability to adapt, to bend rather than break. A flexible spine also encourages the flow of cerebral-spinal fluid as these next activities will illustrate.

Prime Your Sacral Spinal Pump

Would you believe gently rocking back and forth on your tailbone can do great things for your brain? It's true! Your tailbone, i.e. the sacrum, is considered the pump for the cerebral-spinal fluid that moves up your central nervous system and through your brain. This fluid transports nutrients, hormones and neurotransmitters. It also removes toxins from the central nervous system, and cools the brain.

Be self responsible: If you have a back condition, adapt this activity to simply wiggling on a chair.

1. Sit on the floor. Place your hands behind your hips with fingertips pointing forward.

2. Gently lift your feet off the floor and rock back and forth on your tailbone. Rock yourself back and forth as well as in circles until you feel less tense.

Rocking gently on your tailbone helps you loosen up any fixation of the vertebrae after sitting all day, and is good for general body co-ordination. When you feel you have to wiggle in your chair, don't stifle it: Do it! This activity is found both in Brain Gym (called the Rocker™) and Hyperton-X.

Sit on your tailbone and rock gently in a circular motion.

The Energizer™

This activity releases the spine, abdomen and back muscles and can be done easily and safely at your desk. It keeps the spine supple, flexible and relaxed, releasing any fixation of the vertebrae.

1. Put your hands flat on your desk and rest your forehead between your hands, curving your spine. Breathe out all your tension.

2. As you breathe in, scoop your neck forward (imagine pushing a ball with your nose), lifting your head up gently, forehead first, followed by your neck and upper body. Your lower body and shoulders remain relaxed. Lengthen the back, vertebra by vertebra.

3. Exhale as you reverse the process. Bend the spine forward, tucking your chin down into your chest to lengthen the back of your neck, and with a fluid motion scoop your head forward once again, repeating the process several times.

The Energizer was developed for Brain Gym.®

Leg Muscle Release

Here's another activity, this one from *One Brain,* that re-educates the tendon guard response, relaxes the brain stem, and extends your range of motion.

1. Bend and lift your knee as high as you can, bringing your knee toward your chest. Notice the range of motion allowed by your hamstring (the back of your thigh) muscle.

2. Now vigorously pluck the Achilles tendon behind your ankle, between foot and calf muscle. For further muscle relaxation, the calf muscle itself can be pinched inward in the vertical direction of the muscle fibers. As in the spindle cell activation, this is sending a message to your brain to relax these muscles.

THE ENERGIZER ™

1. *Curl forward, head between your hands.*
2. *As you breathe in, scoop your neck forward, gently lifting your head, curving and lengthening your back.*
3. *Exhale as you reverse, bringing your chin to your chest to lengthen the back of your neck.*

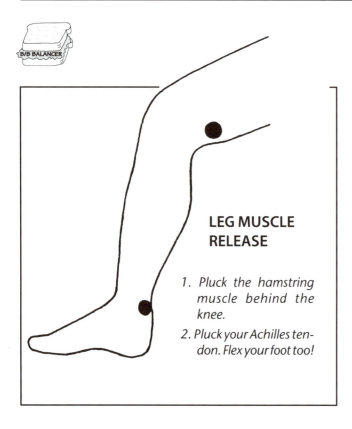

LEG MUSCLE RELEASE

1. Pluck the hamstring muscle behind the knee.

2. Pluck your Achilles tendon. Flex your foot too!

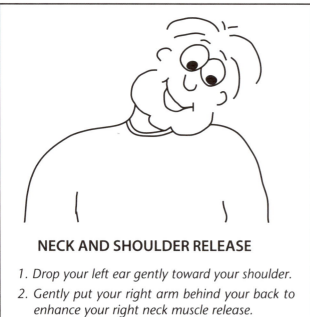

NECK AND SHOULDER RELEASE

1. Drop your left ear gently toward your shoulder.

2. Gently put your right arm behind your back to enhance your right neck muscle release.

3. Next, pluck the hamstring muscle where you can feel two insertions behind the knee, just a few inches up toward the buttock.

4. Lift your knee again and notice if your leg raises higher comfortably. Repeat the plucking/strumming on the muscle until you are aware of increased flexibility. Follow the same steps with your other leg.

Neck and Shoulder Release

The neck is a primary target for stress. We will deal with the neck further in our discussion of hearing, but let's start with this easy release.

1. Let your left ear gently fall toward your left shoulder, only as far as it goes without stress. Your arms rest naturally at your sides.

2. Put your right arm behind your back to enhance the extension you feel in your right neck muscles. Breathe deeply while you hold the position for at least 30 seconds. Repeat on the other side.

3. Gently drop your head to your chest. Slowly rotate your head in a small semi-circle from one shoulder to the other. Hold your extension for a few seconds at any spot that is particularly stressed or tight.

The neck is very vulnerable; never roll your neck completely around in a circle, or make jerking movements. Always move slowly and gently.

Rub Out Tension and Headaches!

Tension headaches are often caused by emotional stress weakening the front neck muscles, which in turn causes back neck muscles to over-contract. To rebalance this blocked body energy, get friendly with these Touch For Health neurolymphatic massage points. If they are sore, rub them gently, increasing the pressure until the "ouch" abates.

1.The **back points** are just where the neck meets the skull on either side of the top vertebra.

2.The **front points** are under the clavicle (collar bone), half way between the breastbone and the tip of the shoulder.

3.The **leg points** are known to relieve headaches due to toxicity. To find these important acupressure points on the gall bladder meridian, stand up and let your arms fall to the side of your thighs. With the middle finger of each hand, probe for a sensitive point as low as you can reach on the side of the leg without bending. Go for the tenderness! If you do not find tenderness (more often the case with men than women) be glad, and stimulate the points anyway. Massage for 7 seconds, and release for 7 seconds, then repeat.

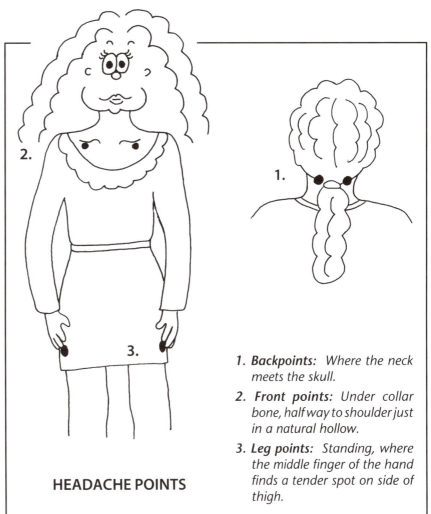

HEADACHE POINTS

1. *Backpoints:* Where the neck meets the skull.

2. *Front points:* Under collar bone, half way to shoulder just in a natural hollow.

3. *Leg points:* Standing, where the middle finger of the hand finds a tender spot on side of thigh.

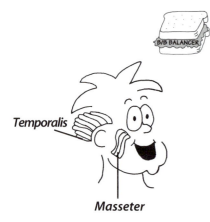

Yawning relaxes your TMJ muscles!

Yawning

Forget what you were taught about yawning. It may not be considered polite, but yawning is good for you! It's your body's way of filling its need for fresh oxygen to energize the brain, getting rid of excess carbon dioxide, and an excellent way to relax tight jaw muscles.

When we're concentrating too hard or under stress, the masseter and temporalis muscles, which control the movement of the jaw, can tighten. This can cause you to grind your teeth at night and can create tension headaches. Many medical and dental issues are attributed to Temporal Mandibular Joint (TMJ for short) problems. There are more nerve endings in the TMJ than in any other joint, and a balanced state is key for sensory processing and self expression.

A few good yawns (you can politely cover your mouth with your hand if you wish) will help relax these muscles and help you avoid any problems. Yawning has also been proven to help detoxify the system, to stimulate tear production (great for dry, stressed eyes) and to relax the body from head to toe.[1] Besides, it just feels good.

So take a deep, noisy, satisfying yawn and massage the joints of your jaws. Your whole body will thank you. Yawning is recommended by all vision enhancement programs, including Janet Goodrich's *Natural Vision Improvement.*

Take a deep, noisy, yawn, inhaling deeply into the diaphragm. Then exhale completely.

Take a deep breath!

Whole therapies have been based around the breathing process. No discussion on breathing would be complete without mentioning the benefits of deep breathing. One of the reasons is because two thirds of the cells that receive oxygen into the blood stream are located in the bottom third of the lungs. So take deep, steady, diaphramatic breaths. You are oxygenating your brain and body with less wear and tear on your lungs and heart, massaging your abdominal organs and stimulating your lymphatic (toxicity removal) system. Make sure your abdomen expands when breathing in and is compressed to empty the lungs when breathing out.

Post-check: Brain/Body

Think of your challenge. Notice your body's physiological responses, and how you feel. Does it differ from your pre-check?

Roleplay the action using your whole body. Does it feel different?

Do some cross march movements, activating both brain hemispheres. Is it easier to do?

Quickly sit down, and repeat the muscle check on your quadriceps muscle.

1. Lift leg and push on thigh—leg should be able to hold.
2. Pinch in belly of muscle, and push down on thigh. Muscle should relax.
3. Pull apart in belly of muscle and muscle check again. Muscle should be strong once more.

Do these checks now show clear messaging between muscle and brain, or do you have to do more integration activity?

❏ Note differences: ❏ Now holds strong when appropriate

                        ❏ Now relaxes when appropriate

❏ **A co-ordination check:** Grasp your nose with your left hand, and reach across your face with your right arm to grasp your left ear. Now switch—left hand grasps right ear, and right hand grasps nose. Switch again, and again. Is it now easier to think and do at the same time?

What differences did you notice from the pre-check?

Are there any responses you would like to improve further?

NOTES

SECTION 9:

SHARPENING YOUR SENSES

"Vision is a learned skill of attention. And, like attention, vision must constantly refocus itself. It moves between near and far, among color, line, and form, between the inner world of dreams, feelings, and thoughts and the outer world of external perceptions.

Vision, for sighted and blind persons alike, is the centering and organizing part of self. Healthy sight requires a fusion of the image seen with the left eye and that seen with the right. Healthy vision depends also on the coordination of seeing with listening, sensing, and balancing skills. Here, the whole of vision is immeasurably greater than the sum of the individual parts."

Gail E. Dennison and Paul E. Dennison, PhD, "Vision, The Centering and Organizing of the Self", *Brain Gym Journal***, Volume VIII, Number 2, Summer 1994**

Section 9:

Sharpening Your Senses

BEING SENSE-ABLE

The next piece in the brain/body integration puzzle is sensory integration. Our brain hemispheres may be integrated, but are our bilateral senses functioning effectively and communicating clearly?

We have already discussed how our cognitive experience of emotion is interpreted in the brain at the amygdala. How then is emotion and stress manifested on the sensory level? Whenever we experience the classic stress response and a circuit lock memory trace of a specific event, the eye direction we were looking in, the way we were hearing, and the muscles firing at the time also lock in our memory circuit with the resulting emotion. If looking in a particular direction is stressful or causes muscle reaction in the body, we know it has to do with what we wanted to see and hear but did not, or what we didn't want to see and hear which was forced upon us at that instant of impact of the event. We can chose to "go blind" or "deaf" rather than deal with the stress of the moment, not allowing optimal processing from that moment forth. Knowing this, we can make a difference in our sensory processing by identifying and releasing the stuck circuits involved in that old memory. Now we can re-educate the stuck circuits involved in our sensory processing.

All the senses must work together, like pieces of a puzzle to create the whole picture.

Coming to your senses

The **sense organs** provide us with all our information about the outside world. They warn us when we are in danger and they feed us the elements of pleasure. They are our interface with our environment, and the first harbingers of the "classic stress response."

In this section we will deal most specifically with improving vision (page 118) and hearing (page122). We will deal with the kinesthetic sense and fine motor coordination in the next section. However, our other senses also figure strongly into the equation and deserve to be mentioned here. The receptors buried in the skin, tongue and nose give us the sense of touch, taste and smell.

Taste and smell are powerful, intertwined triggers. They are called chemosenses, as they both detect chemical molecules.[1] In the case of smell, information goes straight to the emotional centers of the brain without passing through the sensory relay station in the thalamus.[2] No wonder some researchers claim taste and smell are the most immediate senses, and our many likes and dislikes are very much a product of our emotional memories linked to foods and smells. Aside from evoking memories, certain foods have the capacity to stimulate brain activity. Although one man's meat could be another man's poison, it has been found that certain scents such as lemon and peppermint stimulate productive brain activity. Some researchers link milk and starches to relaxation, and cinnamon to male sexual arousal.

Some scents evoke strong emotional memories.

Taste is an extention of smell. It's fascinating that the tongue tastes food on the way in and shapes words on the way out. Its surface is covered with millions of sense organs which process the difference between sweet and sour, salt and bitter. Sweet and salt are registered at the tip of the tongue, sour at the sides, and bitter at the back. Texture of food is also processed. So many of our emotional expressions are couched in the language of taste: Experience can be sweet or bitter; A relationship can be zesty or bland; Life can go down easy, or be hard to digest.

Touch: Our skin is our largest body organ, and being touched and touching provide essential information for our brain's understanding of our world. Touch actually helps us grow, as it stimulates production of acetylcholine (nerve growth factor). Touching on the face and hands is particularly important, where there are lots of nerve nets to feed back to the brain.

Proprioception: There are also sensory receptors in the muscles (you have already met your spindle cells), telling the brain how taut your muscles are, and in what direction they are moving, so that you know where your arms and legs are without looking.

But when we talk about the senses, most of us first think of vision and hearing.

Vision: The eye is like a television camera. Light enters and is focused by the lens to form an upside down image on the darkened back wall of the retina. It is then converted into electrical impulses which are sent to the brain along the optic nerve. It is worth remembering that vision is not a simple by-product of our physical "camera." Only 4% of how we perceive the world is through the eye (sight)—96% we manufacture in the brain (vision).[3]

Hearing: The ear is like a microphone. It picks up sound waves which first vibrate the ear drum, then it mechanically increases the strength of these vibrations approximately 22 times in the middle ear, and passes the sound vibrations in waves through the fluid in the cochlea, moving tiny hairs. This movement converts them into electrical impulses, which are then sent to the brain along the acoustic nerve.

We are each unique in the way we perceive the world, since all sensory input is colored by our beliefs and emotions before we register our final conscious perception of any event. Part of that uniqueness is reflected in our personal brain organization pattern. As we explored in our brain organization profile on page 34, when under stress we revert to a locked stress circuit response—our unintegrated, automatic default setting. Dr. Carla Hannaford, author of *The Dominance Factor* points out our nondominant brain and senses will shut down up to 70% under stress. With brain/body balancers we can unlock these sensory default patterns. Let's learn how to get those senses switched on bilaterally and cooperating at all times, no matter what the life challenge!

Under stress, our non dominant brain shuts down up to 70%.

VISION

When you think about it, it's a miracle we see as well as we do! What we are seeing is actually the product of a sophisticated synthesis of information taking place in our brains, with the brain even filling in the blank spots!

One of the first problems the brain has to deal with is that it receives signals from two eyes at the same time, each one with a slightly different view of the world. The visual cortex processes the information, building up a composite picture by comparing and integrating information from each eye. It must transpose images coming from the eyes, as they are projected upside down on the back of the retina. What's more, just as a computer screen refreshes its image as you move the page, so too the visual image must be constantly refreshed on the rods (light detectors) and cones (color receptors) at the back of your eyes, or we go "blind" to it. For learning to occur, we must not stare at a page: We need to move to stimulate our visual apparatus. Our reward is a heightened visual perception and comprehension.

Each eye has a visual field of about 120°, with an overlap of 60° in the middle where both eyes must co-ordinate as a team for binocular vision. When there is not easy communication between the brain's hemispheres, your eyes will compete for dominance in the area of overlap, switching on and off. Most reading difficulties as well as word and letter reversals are a result of the lack of integration and cooperation in the visual midfield. The two dimensional quality of TV further hinders a child's visual development. As there are developmental differences in children anyway, many normal children do not develop visual co-operation in the midfield until age eight. Until then, reading will be a stressor.

The left eye feeds much of its information into the right (usually whole picture) brain hemisphere, and the right eye feeds the majority of its information into the left (usually logic) brain hemisphere. The two brain hemispheres, in the absence of pathology, are operating in tandem all the time (even though

The eyes have it!

Has this ever happened to you ?

sometimes begrudgingly), with a dominant side going for control.

This simplified schematic shows the individual visual qualities assigned to each brain hemisphere. It also shows the functioning abilities when there is free flowing communication between the two sides. Optimally we want the ability to see all the details within the context of the whole picture, adding in the framework of other sensory information—smell, sound, temperature, etc.

We need to do activities to create stress-free movement in the visual midfield, release near-far focus, and create relaxation to help make seeing easy, stress-free and whole-brained.

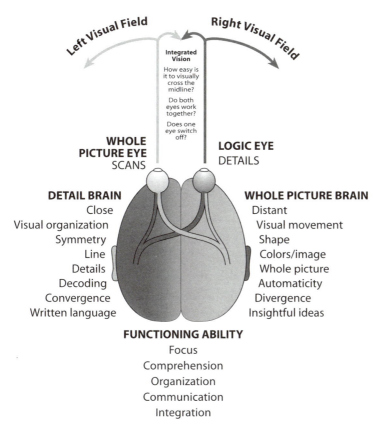

A schematic of how the brain processes vision. When communication is flowing over the corpus callosum, visual information is shared and assimilated from both sides of the brain. We see the whole picture as well as the details.

Pre-check: Vision

See if your eyes are under stress. Check the box if you notice any discomfort, straining or aggravation as you do the following:

❑ Look up ❑ Look down ❑ Look left ❑ Look right
❑ Cover right eye ❑ Cover left eye
❑ Track eyes left to right as if reading (20 times)
❑ Look near ❑ Look far
❑ Wave your hand at the side of your head while looking forward (peripheral vision)
❑ Read aloud ❑ Read silently

ACTIVITIES

Lazy 8s™ for the Eyes

Take a mini vacation for your eyes, to help you read and understand better! Let's do a movement[4] used for years in remedial education to integrate the visual midfield and improve hand-eye coordination.

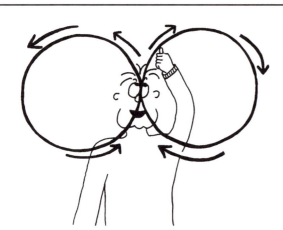

1. Hold your arm in front of you with thumb up.
2. Make a Lazy 8, always going up in the middle.
3. Really extend your eye muscles.
4. Do with each hand, then with both together.

Extend your arm in front of you (about 12-14″ for adults, or 18″ for children), thumb up and level with your nose. Carefully make a Lazy 8 in the air with your eyes focused on your thumb. Always go up in the middle in front of your nose, and down at the sides. Make sure your eyes do the moving—keep your head still and really extend your eye muscles. If you experience strain or discomfort in any eye direction, hold your Positive Points on the forehead, and maintain that position until the stress eases.

Do the Lazy 8 three times with each hand, and three times with both hands clasped together. Repeat until eye movement is smooth. If you want to improve sports performance, hold any small piece of sports equipment (ie racket or ball), in your hand as a focus point for your eyes instead of your thumb!

Eye Points

For a quick visual "pick-me-up", massage your "eye points" at the back of your head, in the hollows above the bony ridge of the lowest turn of your skull (the occipital protuberance). This pressure stimulates your primary visual cortex, which lies directly below. Look in all directions as you rub these hollows on the left and right. Also focus on something close and then on something distant, to activate near/far accommodation.

This short-circuit eye correction is from Three In One Concepts. Once again remember if a specific eye direction is uncomfortable, hold your Positive Points (page 85) until the tension releases.

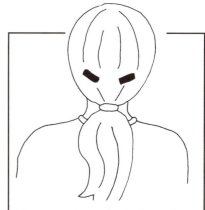

Massage along the indent above the first turn of your skull.

Palming

Whenever your eyes get tired or blurry, rub your hands together to warm them, and then cup your palms over your closed eyes to help stimulate blood circulation. Let your mind relax and visualize a flower or a natural scene to reactivate your creative, pictorial (right) brain hemisphere. Hum or think of music. See how relaxed your eyes feel in a few minutes! This activity is particularly useful when working on a computer. Many vision therapies, if not all, use palming. This activity was sourced from Janet Goodrich's *Natural Vision Improvement*.

Hold the palms of your hands over your eyes.

Post-check: Vision

What differences do you notice? Is there easing of any discomfort or straining as you repeat the following:

- ❏ Look up ❏ Look down ❏ Look left ❏ Look right
- ❏ Cover right eye ❏ Cover left eye
- ❏ Track back and forth as if reading (20 times)
- ❏ Look near ❏ Look far
- ❏ Wave your hand at the side of your head while looking forward (peripheral vision)
- ❏ Read aloud ❏ Read silently

HEARING

To truly understand and comprehend, we must take in the content of what we hear, and perceive it in the context in which it is heard. A cry for help can be a crisis, activating the appropriate survival responses, or it can be a laughing matter, as a friend precariously balances four plates of birthday cake. The statement "You're really something!" can be an insult if it is dripping with sarcasm, or a great compliment when said in sincere admiration. We need both brain hemispheres processing and sharing information to get true meaning. The left hemisphere (usually) is processing the objective content of language –what was said– while the right hemisphere is processing the emotional content of language— how it was said, interpreting facial expressions and body language.[5]

Although about 80% of input from one ear feeds into the opposite brain hemisphere, it does not mean that a person deaf in one ear will never get a balanced message. As long as the brain hemispheres are communicating over the corpus callosum (for which the activities in this book are a key!) auditory information gets passed and shared from one hemisphere to the other, and a balanced auditory message is interpreted. (The same holds true for blindness in one eye: Information is shared between the hemispheres as long as integration is assured, and we get the details in the proper context of the whole picture.)

When we hear something, we are not only activating sensory organs and pathways; we are triggering motor, language, logic and memory circuits. Once again, emotion is a key player: Our thalamus, amygdala and other brain parts are deciding what our emotional (and survival) investment is, and from that whether we are really interested or not. We can tune out what we don't want to hear, or what doesn't fit into our belief system, and tune in what either threatens or pleases us.

Teachers and parents have long known that the admonition "Sit still and listen to me," does not necessarily ensure the listener's full attention and comprehension. Usually the opposite! Indeed,

Has this ever happened to you? We call it selective perception!

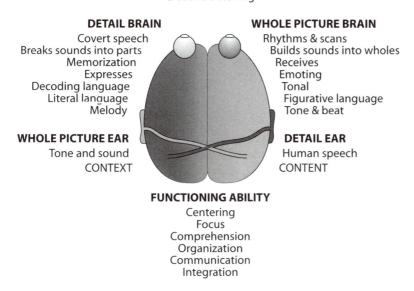

INTEGRATED HEARING
Music & Speech
Language with Meaning
Creative Listening

DETAIL BRAIN
Covert speech
Breaks sounds into parts
Memorization
Expresses
Decoding language
Literal language
Melody

WHOLE PICTURE BRAIN
Rhythms & scans
Builds sounds into wholes
Receives
Emoting
Tonal
Figurative language
Tone & beat

WHOLE PICTURE EAR
Tone and sound
CONTEXT

DETAIL EAR
Human speech
CONTENT

FUNCTIONING ABILITY
Centering
Focus
Comprehension
Organization
Communication
Integration

A schematic of how the brain tends to lateralize hearing, and the benefits of integration. When communication is flowing through the corpus callosum, auditory information is shared and assimilated from both sides of the brain: We can understand and interpret the content, in the emotional context of how it was said.

it is the Educational Kinesiologist's theory that movement is a key to attention and learning.

The vestibular system, which controls our sense of movement and balance, is also centered in the ear. The vestibular system is interconnected to the cerebral cortex, as well as the eyes and core muscles, and is highly important to the learning process. Developmentally, when we don't move and activate the vestibular system, we are not taking in information from the environment.[6]

Our ability to focus and concentrate depends much on our ability to filter out extraneous noises and determine intuitively what is pertinent and what is not. In order to do this we need to feel safe. If we don't feel safe, the brain will stay in survival mode, analyzing all extraneous sounds, constantly on the alert in case of danger. Our awareness is then split and total concentration to higher cortical tasks is impossible. Under these conditions learning is impaired and we may not recall the information later.

Be very aware that our neck is truly on the line for hearing. According to Dr. Dennison, hearing and memory are tied into proprioception in the neck and shoulder muscles. They respond to sound by repositioning the head and ear. Tension in the neck can impact listening, comprehension, thinking, memory, math, spelling and even speaking. So continue to make sure you keep your neck loose and stress-free with short massage breaks and the next activities. These balancers will activate both ears to enhance auditory processing and will re-educate any auditory stuck circuit locks caused by the stress response.

Pre-check: Hearing

As you do these exercises, notice the quality of sound, your comprehension of what you hear, and any body tension. Check boxes for any activities you find difficult.

❏ Turn head to right and listen to sound.
❏ Turn head to left and listen to sound.
❏ Cover over right ear and listen.
❏ Cover over left ear and listen.
❏ Read aloud and notice comfort and quality of tone.
❏ Have someone tell you a 7 digit telephone number and repeat it back to them (activating short-term memory).
❏ Quickly remember what you had for breakfast (activating recent memory).
❏ What was your favorite toy as a child (activating long-term memory).
❏ Add some numbers (activating math).
❏ Have someone ask you to spell a word.

What specific difficulty or discomfort did you notice?

ACTIVITIES

You're All Ears!

Have you ever suddenly realized in the middle of a conversation that you haven't heard a word for several minutes? Whenever your attention wanders, you can get an earful of integration by simply massaging your ears. Gently unroll your ear edges a few times, from top to bottom. Give your ears a gentle tug to the side. Note how it makes sounds seem brighter and clearer. You will notice your attention sharpens and you can both hear and think better.

Dr. John Thie points out that this auricular exercise can also improve range of motion. Turn your head first to one side, and then the other, as far as you can. Then massage your ears, as you gently turn your head again, looking for—and releasing—any stiffness. After you are done, turn your head again, and notice if you are now rotating farther.

When you rub your ears you are actually massaging many different acupressure points which stimulate your whole system for a quick pick-me-up. Massage your ears before you have to speak, write, receive instructions, or just because you like it! Called The Thinking Cap™ in Brain Gym, this activity is used by all the major kinesiologies.

Give your ears a gentle massage, unrolling them as well. Turn your head to release neck stress!

The Owl™

The Owl is designed to release tension in the shoulder and neck muscles and to increase range of motion for turning the head.

1. With your right hand, grasp the top of your left shoulder muscle (the trapezius) and squeeze firmly.

2. Inhale deeply. As you exhale, turn your head away from your hand, to look over your right shoulder. Inhale as you return your head to center.

3. Exhale as you turn your head to look over your left shoulder. Return your head to center.

4. Exhale as you drop your chin to your chest. Inhale as you raise your head. Repeat the three directions, (right, left, down) three times on each side. Then squeeze the left shoulder with the right hand, and repeat the Owl on the other side. This activity is from Brain Gym.

Firmly grasp the trapezius. Breathe out and turn away slowly.

Hyperton-X Neck Release

We know that a blocked muscle either cannot turn on or, conversely, release when appropriate. Here is a good basic technique for releasing a muscle locked in contraction (hypertonic). Deliberately extending the frozen muscle, then activating it against resistance, helps unblock and reset the proprioceptors.

1. Let your left ear fall gently towards your left shoulder as far as it can without strain.

2. Reach over with your left arm to put your hand in position against the right side of your head to provide resistance for step 3.

3. Breathe in, and as you exhale, push your head to the right (10% of your strength for 6 seconds) against your hand which provides light resistance. Rest for a moment and allow your left ear to fall again further toward your left shoulder.

As you breathe out, push for 6 sec., using 10% of your strength, against your hand's light resistance.

Note the increased range of motion. Repeat the neck release two more times. Do the same process three times on the right side. This technique is sourced from Hyperton-X.

Post-check: Hearing

As you repeat these exercises, notice the quality of sound, your comprehension of what you hear, and any body tension. Check box if you desire further improvement.

❏ Turn head to right and listen to sound.

❏ Turn head to left and listen to sound.

❏ Cover over right ear and listen.

❏ Cover over left ear and listen.

❏ Read aloud and notice comfort and quality of tone.

❏ Have someone tell you a 7 digit telephone number, and repeat it back to them (activating short-term memory).

❏ Quickly remember what you had for breakfast (activating recent memory).

❏ What was your favorite toy as a child (activating long-term memory).

❏ Add some numbers (activating math).

❏ Have someone ask you to spell a word.

What improvements have you noted? Is there any area where you desire further improvement?

NOTES

SECTION 10

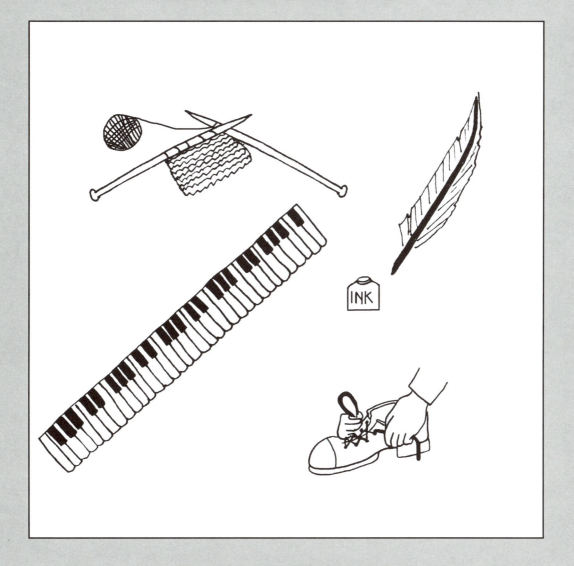

FINE TUNING

"Both (hand and finger) muscle groups are most efficient when they function automatically—when our conscious brain can focus on the content of the message rather than on the vehicle of expression."

Robert Sylwester, *A Celebration of Neurons*, page 69

Section 10:

Fine Tuning

FINE MOTOR

Have you ever had a great idea, picked up a pen to write it down or sketch it, and had the idea disappear as soon as the pen hit the paper? The last piece in the brain/body integration puzzle is fine tuning for fine motor communication. We must remove any blocks to the energy circuits affecting fine motor skills, eye-hand coordination, and the written word. These skills support our successful self expression, be it by knitting, drawing, building, or writing. Expression on a two dimensional sheet of paper combines touch and movement with vision and language. This requires sophisticated skills in perceiving, conceiving, dealing with symbols, expressing, memory and recall. Writing and drawing involve all the domains we have been improving up to now: emotional stress release, brain/body integration, hand-eye coordination, body posture, fine motor skills.[1]

Indeed, in PET scans, the hand area within the brain (particularly the thumb) is most lit up when speaking. Most of our communication is with our body, not our words. So if neural communication between brain and hands is compromised, it makes all communication, including vocalization, more difficult.

Has this ever happened to you?

In the pre TV era, children played endless games of marbles, jacks, pick-up sticks, tiddley winks, etc. All these games developed our ability to focus, concentrate and trained our eye-hand coordination to a high level. Today's children are less active and do not get the same motor skill development from sitting in front of a TV. Less physical activity hinders eye and body development and it's not good for us grown ups either! Back to playing jacks!

Also, consider what a pianist or an opera star does before a concert. They warm up, flex their musical muscles by doing scales. What do you do before you sit down to approach a manual task, or a written assignment? If you are like most, nothing! Rita Edwards, an Educational Kinesiology faculty member from South Africa, in her P.R.E.P.A.R.E. writing program, suggests stimulating our tactile and coordination circuits before writing by using Brain Gym® and other activities. So pick up a piece of paper and clap it aloft between your two hands. Then put a smooth piece of paper in one hand

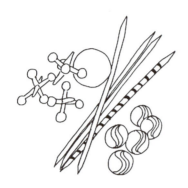

And you thought it was play! It's Introductory Writing and Neurosurgery 001! Back to jacks and pick up sticks!

only and crunch it up into a ball. Smooth it out again with the same hand. Busy fingers, as you figure it out! Now vigorously rub your hands and forearms to stimulate your touch receptors.

Also use a stress ball or playdough to exercise your hands. Take regular breaks from fine motor activities such as writing or typing to move your arms, shoulders, body, and to flex your fingers. Don't let your body energy get stuck: It will result in a stuck brain and stuck creativity.

Why are reading and writing so challenging? Two dimensional written symbols (letters) are not contextual—that is, they are not part of the real, three dimensional world. A three dimensional chair is recognizable whether upright, upside down or sideways. Now consider a two dimensional letter "b". Reversed, it becomes a "d". Upside down, it turns into a "p" and a "q". We need to move these symbols out of the abstract, and make them live comfortably and automatically in our three dimensional bodies. The following activities will help. Although geared to writing, these balancers will improve any fine motor task demanding more dexterity.

Pre-check: Fine Motor

Think of a writing project, and plan what you want to say:

Notice how you feel.

Place 10 coins in a row. Time yourself as you turn over all 10 coins sequentially. How many seconds did it take you?

Write a sentence on a separate piece of paper. Notice the quality of your writing.

Look at the left, middle and right sections of that line. Do any sections feel different? How?

Write the alphabet: abcdef , etc. Do any letters feel awkward?

Do Loops.

ACTIVITIES

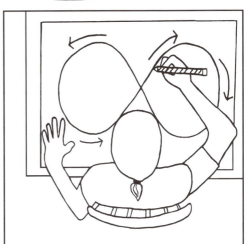

Lazy 8s™ for Writing

Trouble getting started on that project or report? Let your creativity and written expression flow by drawing Lazy 8s on a piece of paper, on the board, or in the sand. Always go up in the middle and down on the side. Use both hands separately and together, and "doodle" different sizes. Drawing the Lazy 8 enables you to cross the visual midline without interruption, thus activating both right and left eyes, and integrating the right and left visual fields. It enhances binocular and peripheral vision and improves eye muscle co-ordination, especially for tracking.

Start in the center. Go up from the center around the top and down on the outside.

The Alphabet 8s™

Whenever your writing looks messy or you feel stuck on a project, practice your alphabet on the Lazy 8. You are taking the two-dimensional, abstract symbols (letters) and grounding them into your body's automatic three dimensional movement in the real world. This will enable you to think creatively and write at the same time, without your body having to think of how to form a particular letter.

After starting with Lazy 8s (above), draw a perpendicular line between the two loops of the "Lazy 8." Fit each lower case letter (print, not cursive) on the Lazy 8, moving up and out from the midline to the left or right. What you are determining: Does the letter "live" to the left or the right of the visual midfield? Without lifting your pen from the paper, each time you print a letter, go back and do a few Lazy 8s, before beginning the next letter again without lifting your pen from the paper. Repeat until there is an automatic flow, and you do not have to think of where to place the letter. This powerful activity from Brain Gym effectively addresses word and letter reversal.

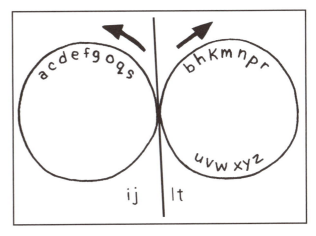

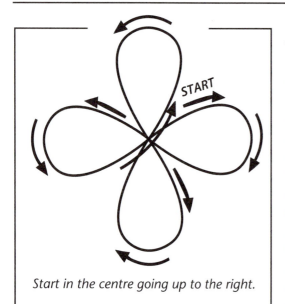

Start in the centre going up to the right.

 # The Cloverleaf™

The Cloverleaf encourages the proper flow for cursive writing, and is a wonderful warm-up to integrate the hand and the eye to move across the midline for non-stressful writing or drawing. Start your cloverleaf pattern by first drawing a horizontal Lazy 8 (page 133) starting in the center, going up toward the right and down and around. When you complete the Lazy 8, start the vertical 8 by first going up to the right, around to the left and down, through the center heading to bottom right, curving around to the left and up to center, where you start a horizontal 8 again. Repeat until it becomes natural and automatic. Start doodling the Cloverleaf! This activity is drawn from the Brain Gym companion course, Vision Gym™.

Post-check: Writing: Notice the Difference

Recommence thinking about your writing project: Notice if it feels easier.

Place 10 coins in a row. Time yourself as you turn over all 10 coins sequentially. Was it easier? Were you faster?

Write another sentence on a separate piece of paper. Notice the quality of your writing. Did it feel easier?

Look at the left, middle and right sections of that line. Do any sections feel different? How?

Write the alphabet: abcdef , etc. Do any letters look and feel different to you?

Do Loops. ℓℓℓℓ

What differences did you notice from your pre-check?

Is there anything you would like to improve further?

SECTION 11

REAL LIFE: HOW TO APPLY
WHAT YOU'VE LEARNED

"Movement is life. It is the door to learning. If learning is defined as "changed behavior," I submit that no learning can take place without movement. Changed Behavior means to have been affected, to be able to perform more precisely, and to have more mastery of a skill. In the brain, movement takes place across synapses which are organized to connect several critical areas necessary for changes of behavior to take place...back brain to front brain, top brain to bottom brain, and left brain hemisphere to right brain hemisphere. Whole-brain learning is the spontaneous interconnection of all the centers of the brain related to the learning event. Whole-brain learning involves physical, emotional, and mental processes that result in permanent changes in skills, attitudes, and behaviors, because the learning is not superficial: it is fully internalized."

Dr. Paul E. Dennison, PhD " A Living Context for Reading",
Brain Gym Journal, **Volume VIII, No.1, Spring 1994.**

Section 11: Real Life:
How to Apply What You've Learned

COMPLETING YOUR PERSONAL PROCESS

T he purpose of this book was to explain how stress impacts your ability to function, how to identify its effects on your learning and performance, and how you can use simple techniques to restore your mental, physical and emotional balance. So let's see if it has truly made a difference, as compared to when you first picked up this book. By doing a post-check, we are anchoring into your brain/body your higher level of functioning in regard to the issues which you identified at the outset.

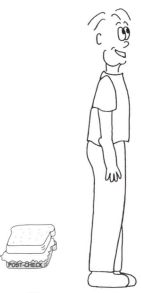

Let us once again think of the stressful situation you noted on page 32 and analyzed on pages 46 and 47, and do our Noticing process.

Stand comfortably and think of the situation that challenged your brain/body system. *Now objectively notice how your body is reacting, remembering there are no rights or wrongs, just what is. This gives you a measure of any differences achieved as a result of our Integrating Activities.*

Notice your posture in relation to the floor: (e.g. upright, swaying forward, backward or sideways)

Any tension, pain or weakness in your body? Where is it? (e.g. legs, back, shoulders, neck, stomach, chest, heart, throat, jaw) Any differences?

Look at an object straight ahead. Is it clear or blurry? Any difference in how your eyes are processing?

Listen to a sound in the room. Are you hearing equally through both ears? Is there a difference in tonality or comprehension?

Lift your arms 30º up in front of body. Is that easy or does it take energy?

Hold your arms there for 30 seconds. Is it easy or stressful?

Go back to the pre-check on page 32 and notice your areas of improvement, which indicate the freeing of old blocked circuit patterns. Are you satisfied, or does further work need be done before proceeding to new goals?

Hey! The world looks much better now!

It's easier to hold up my arms!

USING YOUR TOOLS THE SIMPLEST WAY

By virtue of the fact you are still reading this book, we assume you have had a first hand experience of the simple change for the better possible with these techniques. Hopefully *Making the Brain/Body Connection* has lived up to its subtitle and presented you with the tools you need to release your mental, physical and emotional blocks to success. But tools are just that—tools only. If you leave them in the tool chest, they are just useless pieces of inert material. Let's make sure that you know how to pick them up and use them!

On the simplest level, if you commit to regularly doing the Quick Six activities reviewed on page 140, you will be ahead of the pack in maintaining a calm, balanced state. Take these individual activities with you into your real life, adapting them to fit into your home and work environments. Always keep a water glass or bottle handy, for little sips throughout the day. As soon as you start to feel fuzzy-brained, take a sip of water, take a deep breath, and reach up to casually massage your "plugging in" energy points (page 58), first on one side of your breast bone, then the other. From time to time, reach up and massage your eye points (page 121), first one side, then the other. Do the same for your ears, casually massaging one, then later, the other. At best, nobody will notice at all. At worst, people will think you are itchy. No one will know you are constantly managing your state with superb body management techniques.

You can do the cross patterning activity on page 103 unobtrusively anywhere—in a waiting room, an exam, a meeting— reactivating your brain hemispheres by simply flicking an opposite finger and toe, using minute movements. Your brain is firing off the circuits for brain/body integration, even without big gestures.

Modify your Cook's Hook Up (page 59), by comfortably crossing your arms and legs, without actually grasping the ball of your foot. Nobody knows your tongue is on the roof of your mouth, unless you try to talk! Then the second part—feet flat on the floor, and fingertips together. People use this method all the time. It's an instinctive stance for energy balancing and stress release.

The same is true for Emotional Stress Release (Positive Points): hand on the forehead, very lightly. People do this instinctively—the "Oh, no!" response of hand to the head. All we have to remember is to do it deliberately, and to hold our hand in place. It's easy when we're seated at a desk or table. No one will look twice. Write tests or work to deadline with one hand on your forehead.

Simply continue to work on clearing up your processing blocks, for ever increasing ease and effectiveness. Also maintain your gains by using the Quick Six, and any choice of the brain/body balancers. On the next page we review the Quick Six—the very minimum support for whole brain/body functioning. On page 141 we offer suggestions of how you might choose to incorporate other brain/body balancers into your life.

This is the simplest way of working with the tools—just choosing individual activities you like as you think of it, to rebalance yourself in the moment as life's stressors impact your well-being.

The next step and degree of commitment is for you to choose to embark on a deliberate re-education of your brain/body system for a specific task or issue. Specialized Kinesiologists call that balancing for a goal. We have put together a simple model for you, to make it easy to tackle bigger issues in more depth. Even in the context of this larger format, you are free to pick and choose what areas of exploration you feel will be most revealing and useful to you. Trust your intuition, and just go for it!

Mental rehearsal always paves the way.

THE QUICK SIX IN REVIEW

1. Drink Water
(page 57)

2. Plug In
(page 58)

3. Cross Patterning
(page 103)

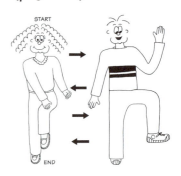

4. Cook's Hook Up
(page 59)

5. Positive Points
(page 85)

6. Be Sense-able
(pages 121 & 125)

 If you do no more, at least do these six simple, unobtrusive activities to support your brain/body system. No excuses!

OTHER SUGGESTIONS FOR DAILY USE

In the Morning

- ❑ Quick Six
- ❑ Positive Points to Preview Your Day
- ❑ Rub Gait Points on the Feet

Studying and Tests

- ❑ Quick Six
- ❑ Positive Points and Mental Rehearsal
- ❑ Lazy 8s for the Eyes
- ❑ Alphabet 8s for Writing

Work at Computer Terminals

- ❑ Quick Six
- ❑ Sacral Spinal Rock
- ❑ Energizer
- ❑ Lazy 8s for the Eyes
- ❑ Palming
- ❑ Owl & Neck Release
- ❑ Hyperton-X Release

Work Towards Goals & Affirmations

- ❑ Cook's Hook Up
- ❑ Emotional Stress Release
- ❑ Eye Rotation

Back Care

- ❑ Appropriate Exercise as Suggested by a Licensed Professional
- ❑ Rub Gait Points
- ❑ Energizer
- ❑ Owl & Neck Release
- ❑ Hyperton-X Release
- ❑ Leg Muscle Release

Before Sports

- ❑ Quick Six
- ❑ Positive Points and Mental Rehearsal
- ❑ Gait Points
- ❑ Sacral Spinal Rock
- ❑ Leg Muscle Release
- ❑ Appropriate Stretches

Reading

- ❑ Quick Six
- ❑ Lazy 8s for the Eyes
- ❑ Eye Points
- ❑ Palming
- ❑ Lazy 8s for Writing
- ❑ Energizer
- ❑ Owl & Neck Release
- ❑ Leg Muscle Release

Top **10 Brain/Body Integrators**

1. Drink Water
2. Plug In
3. Cross Marching
4. Cook's Hook Up
5. Positive Points
6. Gait Points
7. Sacral Spinal Pump
8. Lazy 8s for Eyes
9. You're All Ears
10. Alphabet 8s

Top **10 Stress Releasers**

1. Drink Water
2. Plug In
3. Cross Marching
4. Polarized Breathing
5. Cook's Hook Up
6. Positive Points
7. Eyes Around the Clock
8. Anchoring
9. Rub Eye Points & Ears
10. Rub Out Headaches

REMEMBER TO NOTICE THE DIFFERENCE!

PUTTING IT ALL TOGETHER

Y ou now have all the necessary ingredients for successfully unlocking the blocks to future learning and performance goals. Let's put it all together in a simple ten-step format so you can easily apply what you have learned to other life challenges. Here is a synthesis of the model, after which I'll present you with forms to make applying the model to any challenge as easy as 1, 2, 3!

1. Start off from a balanced state using The Quick Six, or other integrating techniques.

2. Choose a clear, positive goal that fits the issues in your life. It's the best investment you can make!

1. Start off from a balanced state.

Attempting to learn from a stressed state, only anchors in more stress responses. Use *The Quick Six* (or other brain/body balancers of your choosing), to bring yourself into a centered and calm state from which you can safely and comfortably consider further life challenges. We reviewed The Quick Six on page 140, and gave you easy applications for other brain/body balancers on page 141.

2. Have a clear, positive goal.

Next identify a clear, positive goal you wish to achieve. It can be a little one: Small changes can be a catalyst for amazing break-throughs. In Section 2 we asked you to take a look at your non-serving behaviors, and also asked you to identify the good reasons you bought this book. Throughout the book you identified areas where your functioning could be improved, and identified key stressors in your life which can also be valuable to address and defuse. Choose some of these issues to improve. We also encourage you to spend time on additional goal setting on page 147 when you feel ready, as it is our intent to leave you with both the desire for moving forward in your life, as well as the tools for achieving it. Setting your goals is the most positive investment you can make in yourself and your future.

3. Release your unwillingness to change.[1]

You need a true willingness to experience change. Often subconscious sabotage patterns are the real blocks to achieving success. Indeed, it has been proven time and time again, that most people are not afraid of failure: Most of us are terrified of achieving success, and releasing stress around the issue of being "good enough" is useful. Before you work on changing a behavior or going for a goal itself, it pays to honestly evaluate the pros and cons of any positive change you are considering. You will need to re-educate your response to any fears you have about how getting your goal will affect you and your relationships. Remember, we discovered that any change, even good change, is stressful, and should be handled. Stress releasing the affirmations on page 149 with Positive Points and Eye Rotations is a good start.

3. Release your unwillingness to change.

4. Visualize achieving your goal, and roleplay a relevant action.

As well as experiencing your goal in your mind's eye, also activate the physical circuits that have to support you in achieving it. This can be a literal roleplay, like a golf swing if your goal is to improve your golf game. It can be a symbolic gesture if your goal is something more abstract, such as self acceptance. If that were the goal, you could give yourself a symbolic hug, or pretend to open a door and walk through it into a room full of that positive state.

4. Visualize achieving your goal, and also roleplay a relevant action.

5. Get a clear objective assessment of your current functioning in regard to your goal, with Noticing or, if you know how, muscle checking.

You must clearly and consciously identify all the ways your brain/body is currently not supporting you in achieving that goal: Noticing or muscle checking provides **a personal evaluation system** to identify areas of behavior and function which are holding you back from being the best you can be. Use the subtle pre-checking activities that follow on pages 150-152 to distinguish your body's regular stuck circuit locks.

5. See how your brain/body is currently supporting you in the light of your goal.

*6. Embrace uncertainty:
Often a sense of confusion
occurs before a higher level of
integration is reached.*

*7. Use brain/body balancers to
help you get the job done!*

*8. Anchor improvement with
the post check:
Do you feel better?
Are you more effective?
Are things easier?*

6. Be willing to embrace uncertainty.

Change demands that we pull ourselves out of our old homeostasis—the way we respond to life and challenge—and allow ourselves to temporarily **embrace uncertainty** as our body/brain learns a better way to handle itself. Often this manifests as a feeling of confusion or spaciness, which you should recognize as a transitory stage of the change process, a stage you move through by using brain/body balancing activities (see #7), and allowing integration time. Learn to recognize this state, and to give yourself time and personal attention to move through it, never driving or otherwise jeopardizing yourself if you feel spacey.

7. Use your brain/body re-education techniques to get the job done.

It's not enough to know about them: Commit yourself to using the re-education tools you now have to take your brain/body system to a higher level of functioning—its new homeostasis. This book has provided you with a wonderful assortment of specific brain/body balancers, and we invite you to use other systems you already know. It might be a hobby, sport or therapy, or be as simple as a walk or singing a song—whatever works to help you relax and achieve focus. Modalities that couple slow, intentional movement with balanced, graceful flow are particularly suitable, such as yoga, tai-chi and dance. An important awareness is that you're using the modality **intentionally to re-create a normal free flowing brain/body response in the face of a specific stressor**. Think of your stressor or goal as you perform balancing activities. You are re-educating your response—not simply escaping from the stressful situation to do something you like better!

8. Post-check to anchor in the new learning.

To assure that change has truly occurred, you need to **anchor** the brain/body's recognition and acceptance of the new learning. Repeat all the pre-checks, using noticing and/or muscle checking, and compare your brain/body response. Have you achieved the level of new integration that you desire? If so, you are done, and are free to move toward your goal with a new level of brain/body support for your conscious intent.

9. Commit to an action plan and maintenance.

9. Act on your goal, and maintain your newly won integration.

In the face of real life challenges to your newly won brain, body and sensory integration, it pays to build in a "maintenance" plan which includes using brain/body balancers to maintain your new-found ease of functioning. Reactivating the new circuits deepens their myelination and reinforces long-term memory. It also pays to "check in" from time to time, to see if the stressors of daily life have caused you to slip out of your optimal state. If you notice that you have, take care of it with the brain/body balancers!

10. Celebrate your accomplishment.

10. Celebrate!

Acknowledge what has become easier or is flowing more smoothly. Celebration and joy lowers stress and raises the levels of serotonin in the brain to make everything easier yet!

USE THE FOLLOWING PAGES TO TAKE YOU STEP BY STEP TOWARDS ANY NEW CHALLENGE OR GOAL.

10 STEP CHANGE PROCESS: SUMMARY SHEET

1. Put myself in balanced state with Quick Six and _____

2. My goal is to clear stress around (p.147)_____

3. Willingness to benefit with Quick Six, and Emotional Stress Release (p.149)_____

4. Visualize and activate my goal with this roleplay(p.150)_____

5. Do Prechecks pages (150-152). My areas of imbalance are:
   ❏ Electromagnetic ❏ Emotional ❏ Brain/Body Integration ❏ Vision ❏ Hearing ❏ Fine Motor

I noticed _____

6. I am willing to embrace change and allow time and space for process (p. 153)_____

7. I will start to clear this issue with the Quick 6 and will add these other activities (p. 153)

Electromagnetic
❏ Drink Water
❏ Plug In for Balanced Energy
❏ Cook's Hook Up
❏ Polarized Breathing

Brain/Body Integration
❏ Cross Patterning
❏ Gait Points
❏ Sacral Spinal Pump
❏ The Energizer
❏ Leg Muscle Release
❏ Neck & Shoulder Release
❏ Rub Out Tension & Headaches

Emotional
❏ Emotional Stress Release
❏ Eye Rotations
❏ Anchoring

Hearing
❏ Rub Ears
❏ The Owl
❏ Hyperton-X Neck Release

Vision
❏ Lazy 8s for the Eyes
❏ Eye Points
❏ Palming

Fine Motor
❏ Lazy 8s for Writing
❏ Alphabet 8s
❏ Cloverleaf

8. Do Post-checks on pages 154-156. Note improvements_____

_____ I am satisfied with my new level of functioning. ❏ Yes ❏ No

If you checked "yes" your work is complete. If you checked "no" simply repeat steps 6-8, adding new balancing activities until you achieve your desired level of improvement.

9. I'll do my action plan and choose maintenance activities on page 157.

10. I'll celebrate my new learning by (p.158)_____

1. START FROM A BALANCED STATE

Use the Quick 6, other Brain/Body Balancers, or other activities from your own knowledge such as tai-chi, yoga, a walk, a bath: whatever puts you into whole brain/body integration, and a sense of well being. Remember to seek a comfortable location, free from distraction if possible.

I will begin by:_____

_____

2. HAVE A CLEAR, POSITIVE GOAL

Your goal can be as simple as continuing to work on clearing the stress responses you noticed as you read this book. Once you are satisfied, you will want to identify profitable life issues to address. Most people are so busy treading water, they're not clear in what direction they should be swimming. It's important to know where you intend to go, so that your mind and body can work together to get you there! If nothing else, consider the tombstone test. When you die, what do you want people to say your life stood for? What do you really value in your life?

_____

_____

_____

What is it I really want?

Although simplistic, this tombstone test provides a litmus test for what is, and is not, important to your long-term goals. You can start immediately, removing and reducing irrelevant stressors, people, and expectations from your life that don't support your true life purpose. Take a stand! Don't say yes to all requests for volunteer tasks, or invitations by people you really don't like. Consider your time and energy as commodities which must be valued and used for your own ends. Use the stress management techniques you have learned in this book to make it easy to do so.

S.M.A.R.T. Goal Setting[3]

Remember to make a goal:

1) **S**pecifically stated—clear and positive

2) **M**easurable—so you can evaluate your progress

3) **A**ttainable—a reasonable time frame to attain the goal

4) **R**ealistic—you can reasonably achieve the goal

5) **T**imetabled—back it up with an action plan

Now we will share with you a simple model for long-term goal setting, to help you determine what goals will best support your life purpose. It is our recommendation that you take chunks of time to consider each of the areas that support a well-balanced life. Don't be overwhelmed with the task. Divide and conquer, knowing that ultimately you will have a brilliant new insight into what it is you really want, knowing you now have acquired effective tools to help you achieve it.

Consider your personal long-term goals. You should identify at least one from each of these categories. Chunk down the assignment, to complete it at your own convenience.

Career:

Family & Social:

Physical (exercise programs, hiking etc.):

Financial:

Self-improvement (travel, education, hobbies etc.):

Spiritual:

For effective goal setting, one must set out a timeline for breaking down the task into manageable chunks. If you want to achieve a specific goal within 5 years, what has to be in place 1 year hence? For that to take place, what has to be done in 1 month? To facilitate that, what preliminaries do you need to do this week? Big goals get accomplished one baby step at a time! For more on goal setting see Wayne Topping's *Success Over Distress*, p. 67, and *Wishcraft* by Barbara Sheir.

3. BEING WILLING TO BENEFIT

Use positive affirmations and statements to help stress release your willingness to let the process be easy. So often we sabotage ourselves because of issues of self-worth. Work with these statements, or make up positively worded statements around your goal issue, noticing the impact they have on your brain/body. Defuse with Positive Points, eye rotations and other integrating activities. Think about the statement again, and notice any improvements in brain/body reaction. The following affirmations were sourced from Dr. Wayne Topping's *Success Over Distress* and *Stress Release*.

Self Esteem

1. I like myself.
2. I love myself.
3. I love myself unconditionally.
4. I am a worthwhile person.
5. I deserve praise, admiration and respect.

Finances

1. I am successful.
2. People are happy to pay me.
3. I no longer believe it is wrong to be wealthy.
4. I no longer have to go along with limiting ideas about making and having money.
5. I deserve financial abundance.

Procrastination

1. People approve of me.
2. I am successful.
3. I accept the consequences of my decisions.
4. It's OK to experience anxious feelings.
5. I complete what I start.

Success

1. I am proud of my achievements.
2. I have plenty of energy to accomplish what I want to do.
3. I have determination, drive and self-confidence.
4. I enjoy getting things done.
5. I deserve to be successful.

Goal Setting

1. I set goals easily.
2. I automatically think in a decisive and determined way.
3. I enjoy being responsible.
4. I know what I want out of life.
5. I have the power to live my dreams.

Weight Loss

1. I eat to live.
2. I believe I can lose weight.
3. I want to lose weight.
4. I like my body.
5. I am worthy of a good figure.

4. ACTIVATE THE GOAL: VISUALIZE IT & ROLEPLAY A RELEVANT ACTION

I imagine:

1.

2.

I do:

1.

2.

5. ASSESS YOUR CURRENT FUNCTIONING: THE PRE-CHECK

General pre-checks

1. After doing a physical activity pertaining to your goal, and thinking of your goal, objectively notice how your body is reacting. Remember, there are no rights or wrongs, just what is. Notice your posture in relation to the floor. (e.g. upright, swaying forward, backwards or sideways)

2. Notice any tension, pain or weakness in your body. Where is it? (eg legs, back, shoulders, neck, stomach, chest, throat, jaw)

3. Look at an object straight ahead. Is it clear or blurry?

4. Listen to a sound in the room. Is it tinny or resonant? Are you hearing equally through both ears?

5. Lift your arms 30 º up in front of your body. Is that easy or does it take effort? ❏ Easy   ❏ Difficult

6. Hold your arms there for 30 seconds. Is it easy or difficult? ❏ Easy   ❏ Difficult

7. Jot down what you feel are the most interesting responses you noticed in your body when you both thought of your challenge or goal, and when you acted it out.

Now that you have looked at your body's general responses, move on to more specific pre-checks of your choosing.

Electromagnetic

1. Are you alert? ❏ Yes ❏ No

2. Do you have focus? ❏ Yes ❏ No

3. Is your concentration and comprehension good? ❏ Yes ❏ No

4. Does your head feel clear? ❏ Yes ❏ No

5. Do you feel relaxed? ❏ Yes ❏ No

Brain/Body

1. Do some cross march movements, opposite arm and leg moving.

2. Quickly sit down and muscle check your quadriceps.

   a.   Lift leg and push on thigh. Is the muscle able to hold strong? ❏ Yes ❏ No

   b.   Pinch in belly of muscle, and push down on thigh. Is the muscle able to relax?. ❏ Yes ❏ No

   c.   Pull apart in belly of muscle and muscle check again. Is the muscle strong? ❏ Yes ❏ No

3. A coordination check: Grasp your nose with your left hand, and reach across your face with your right arm to grasp your left ear. Now switch—left hand grasps right ear, and right hand grasps nose. Switch again. Is it easy or difficult to think and do at the same time? ❏ Easy   ❏ Difficult

Emotional Stress

1. Think of a stressful situation in relation to your specific goal. Note your body's physical reactions when you visualize the emotionally stressful situation.

Vision

Make a checkmark in the boxes where you notice any discomfort, straining or aggravation as you do the following:

❏ Look up ❏ Look down ❏ Look left ❏ Look right

❏ Cover right eye ❏ Cover left eye

❏ Track back and forth, following your thumb with your eyes as when reading (20 times).

❏ Look near ❏ Look far

❏ Wave at the side of your head while looking forward (peripheral vision).

❏ Read aloud ❏ Read silently

Hearing

As you do these checks, notice the quality of sound, your comprehension of what you hear, and any body tension. Check boxes of any activities you find difficult.

❏ Turn head to right and listen to sound.

❏ Turn head to left and listen to sound.

❏ Cover over right ear and listen. ❏ Cover over left ear and listen.

❏ Read aloud and notice comfort and quality of tone.

❏ Have someone tell you a 7 digit telephone number, and repeat it back to them (activating short-term memory).

❏ Quickly remember what you had for breakfast (activating recent memory).

❏ What was your favorite toy as a child (activating long-term memory).

❏ Add some numbers (activating math).

❏ Have someone ask you to spell a word.

Fine Motor

1. Think of a writing project, and start it: Notice how you feel.

2. Write a sentence on a separate piece of paper. Notice the quality of your writing.

3. Look at the left, middle and right sections of that line. Do any sections feel different? How?

4. Write the alphabet: abcdef etc. Do any letters feel awkward?

5. Do loops. *llll*

6. BE WILLING TO EMBRACE UNCERTAINTY

Remember that a feeling of spaciness is possible as you identify the need for improved neural connections and brain/body integration. Give yourself the time and space to safely regain focus and clarity, using the balancers below, or any other form of self-care (including sleep!) that your body calls for.

I will allow myself the time and space to:

7. USE YOUR BRAIN/BODY BALANCERS TO GET THE JOB DONE

Choose from the various techniques we have shared with you in this book, or use what feels right for you from your own knowledge. Then repeat Step 4, the visualization and roleplay, and note any new ease of functioning.

Electromagnetic
- ❏ Drink Water
- ❏ Plug In for Balanced Energy
- ❏ Cook's Hook Up
- ❏ Polarized Breathing

Brain/Body Integration
- ❏ Cross Patterning
- ❏ Gait Points
- ❏ Sacral Spinal Pump
- ❏ The Energizer
- ❏ Leg Muscle Release
- ❏ Neck and Shoulder Release
- ❏ Rub Out Tension & Headaches
- ❏ Yawning

Hearing
- ❏ Rub Ears
- ❏ The Owl
- ❏ Hyperton-X Neck Release

Emotional
- ❏ Emotional Stress Release
- ❏ Eye Rotations
- ❏ Anchoring

Fine Motor
- ❏ Lazy 8s for Writing
- ❏ Alphabet 8s
- ❏ Cloverleaf

Vision
- ❏ Lazy 8s for the Eyes
- ❏ Eye Points
- ❏ Palming

8. ANCHORING IN THE NEW LEARNING - THE POST-CHECK

Electromagnetic

1. Are you more alert? ❏ Yes ❏ No

2. Do you have better focus? ❏ Yes ❏ No

3. Is your concentration and comprehension better? ❏ Yes ❏ No

4. Does your head feel more clear? ❏ Yes ❏ No

5. Do you feel more relaxed? ❏ Yes ❏ No

6. Are you free of physical signs of stress? ❏ Yes ❏ No

Brain/Body

1. Think of the challenge. Notice your body's responses, and how you feel. Does it differ from your pre-check?

2. Roleplay the action related to your goal using your whole body. Does it feel different?

3. Do some cross march movements, opposite arm and leg moving. Is it any easier?

4. Quickly sit down and repeat muscle check on the quadriceps. Check "yes" or "no" for the questions.

   a. Lift leg and push on thigh. Is the muscle able to hold strong? ❏ Yes ❏ No

   b. Pinch in belly of muscle, and push down on thigh. Is the muscle able to relax? ❏ Yes ❏ No

   c. Pull apart in belly of muscle and muscle check again. Is the muscle strong? ❏ Yes ❏ No

5. A coordination check: Grasp your nose with your left hand, and reach across your face with your right arm to grasp your left ear. Now switch—left hand grasps right ear, and right hand grasps nose. Switch again. Is it easier to think and do at the same time? ❏ Yes ❏ No

6. Have these checks shown there is now clear messaging between muscle and brain, or do you have to do more integration? ❏ Yes ❏ No

I need more integration re:_____

Emotional Stress

1. Think of your stressful situation again. Note the differences and improvements in your reaction to the stressor. Is there a difference in how you feel emotionally?

I notice:

Vision

Make a checkmark in the boxes where you notice any discomfort, straining or aggravation as you do the following:

❑ Look up ❑ Look down ❑ Look left ❑ Look right

❑ Cover right eye ❑ Cover left eye

❑ Track back and forth as when reading (20 times).

❑ Look near ❑ Look far

❑ Wave at the side of your head while looking forward (peripheral vision).

❑ Read aloud ❑ Read silently

What differences do you notice?

Hearing

As you do these exercises, notice the quality of sound, your comprehension of what you hear, and any body tension. Check boxes of any activities you find difficult. Do you notice any differences?

❑ Turn head to right and listen to sound.

❑ Turn head to left and listen to sound.

❑ Cover over right ear and listen. ❑ Cover over left ear and listen.

❑ Read aloud and notice comfort and quality of tone.

❑ Have someone tell you a 7 digit telephone number, and repeat it back to them (activating short term memory).

❑ Quickly remember what you had for breakfast (activating recent memory).

❑ What was your favorite toy as a child (activating long-term memory).

❑ Add some numbers (activating math).

❑ Have someone ask you to spell a word.

Fine Motor

1. Recommence your writing project. Does it feel easier?

2. Write a sentence on a separate piece of paper. Notice the quality of your writing.

3. Look at the left, middle and right sections of that line. Do any sections feel different? How?

4. Write the alphabet: abcdef etc. Do the letters look or feel different to you?

5. Do loops.

6. I want to see more improvement. ❏ Yes ❏ No

7. I need to do more Brain/Body Balancers. ❏ Yes ❏ No

General post-checks

1. Stand comfortably and think of your challenge or goal once again. Now objectively notice what your body is doing, remembering there are no rights or wrongs, just what is. Note any differences to your pre-check reactions. Notice your posture in relation to the floor. (e.g. upright, swaying forward, backwards or sideways)

2. Notice if any tension, pain or weakness remains in your body. Where is it? (eg. legs, back, shoulders, neck, stomach, chest, throat, jaw)

3. Look at an object straight ahead. Is it clear or blurry?

4. Listen to a sound in the room. Is it tinny or resonant? Are you hearing equally through both ears?

5. Lift your arms 30 º up in front of your body. Is that easy or does it take effort? ❏ Easy ❏ Difficult

6. Hold your arms there for 30 seconds. Is it easy or difficult? ❏ Easy ❏ Difficult

7. Jot down what you feel are the most interesting responses you noticed in your body when you did your post-check. What do they mean?

Are there any body responses you wish to work on further at this time? Using what techniques?

9. MY PERSONAL ACTION PLAN

1. My goal is to clear any remaining stress around:

2. How I want to feel inside myself:

3. How I want to change my behavior in relationship to the old triggers:

4. My course of action: what I am willing to do

5. I will use these brain/body balancers to make it easy to support my new-found integration:

Electromagnetic
- ❏ Drink Water
- ❏ Plug In for Balanced Energy
- ❏ Cook's Hook Up
- ❏ Polarized Breathing

Brain/Body Integration
- ❏ Cross Patterning
- ❏ Gait Points
- ❏ Sacral Spinal Rock
- ❏ The Energizer
- ❏ Leg Muscle Release
- ❏ Neck & Shoulder Release
- ❏ Rub Out Tension & Headaches
- ❏ Yawning

Hearing
- ❏ Rub Ears
- ❏ The Owl
- ❏ Hyperton-X Neck Release

Emotional
- ❏ Emotional Stress Release
- ❏ Eye Rotations
- ❏ Anchoring

Fine Motor
- ❏ Lazy 8s for Writing
- ❏ Alphabet 8s
- ❏ Cloverleaf

Vision
- ❏ Lazy 8s for the Eyes
- ❏ Eye Points
- ❏ Palming

6.   I will use them _____ times. (Number of times a day--3 is average.)

     I will continue for _____ weeks. (Number or weeks–3 weeks is good for habit change.)

7. I will periodically check in to make sure new stressors have not compromised my integration.

8. I want to note and remember that a related area I may choose to work on next is:

10. CELEBRATE YOUR ACCOMPLISHMENT

As well as stepping up production of your "feel good" chemical messengers, the ritual of a celebration further anchors in your new heightened ability and brain/body communication. It can be as simple as a high five or an affirmative "Yes!" So take a moment for self acknowledgment!

I will celebrate my improvements by :

I will keep track of all the steps of my change process on the summary sheet on page 146.

RE-APPLY THESE STEPS TO ANY NEW CHALLENGE OR GOAL

When you feel ready, willing and able, start at number one again with your next chosen step toward better functioning. Life is a process, so why not make it an upward evolution? By constantly being consciously aware of how we act and react in the world, we can re-educate our brain/body to become more effective!

Keep in mind that lifelong, familiar patterns of unserving mental, physical and emotional locks can be triggered again and again by a related stressor, until our new balanced functioning becomes the familiar brain/body response. Don't be discouraged. You can choose to seek out professional assistance or study more advanced techniques to deal with those past issues more quickly and on a deeper level, if you desire. In the meantime, the improvement process has begun, and you are on your way.

The one price you must be willing to pay by assuming personal responsibility for your functioning is that you give up your victim status. You need never again say: "That's just the way I am. I just can't do better !" You can step into higher functioning and you *can* get better. Simple, effective and powerful help lies in these pages. It's up to you to have the self-responsibility and desire to implement it. Once you do, and feel the difference, it's our hope you will seek out even deeper answers with additional training.

Our reference section can assist you on your continued journey. Bon Voyage!

SECTION 12

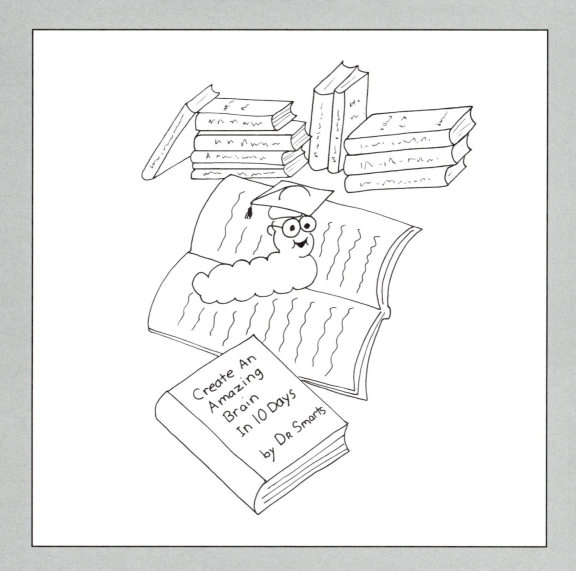

REFERENCE

"We can change cellular memory whenever we make the choice to do so, both psychologically and physically. Just as we can retrain muscle cells for new function, we can retrain memory neurons in the brain."

Gordon Stokes and Daniel Whiteside, *Tools of the Trade,* page 72

Section 12:

Reference

YOU CAN GET THERE FROM HERE

What comes next? If you choose, you could benefit from more self exploration and learning new skills in the areas of:

- Personal Organization
- Sensory Integration
- Time Management
- Physical Fitness
- Nutritional Education
- Brain Based Learning
- Long & Short Term Goal Setting and Plans of Action

You will find the bookshelves full of good resources to support further personal work. I particularly recommend Dr. Wayne Topping's *Success Over Distress,* for an introductory kinesiological workshopping of the above areas, and Dennison's *Brain Gym, Teacher's Edition,* for more on brain/body integration activities.

Classes in Brain Gym, Touch For Health, Three In One Concepts, Wellness Kinesiology (see page 162 for sources) or Lightning Learning (page 174) are exciting routes to self-discovery and enhanced performance. All courses in Specialized Kinesiology teach simple yet profound techniques for switching on the brain/body connection for enhanced functioning.

Classes in Specialized Kinesiology allow you to move quickly through identifying and releasing imbalances that may be influencing your mental, physical and emotional well-being.

All association certified courses teach muscle checking as a means to provide biofeedback from the brain and central nervous system. As already described, muscle checking provides a stress/non stress read-out of mental, physical and emotional energetic imbalances.

For an instructor near you, contact one of the organizations listed on pages 162-164. **Assume personal responsibility in checking the experience and credential of any instructor to whom you are referred, as these are membership organizations rather than licensing bodies.**

EDUCATIONAL OPPORTUNITIES

If you want to learn more about Specialized Kinesiology, contact one or more of the organizations below.

Brain Gym® (Educational Kinesiology)

Brain Gym was chosen as one of 12 exemplary programs "that model excellence in the classroom and have demonstrated effective results" by a White House Task Force on Innovative Learning, Washington D.C. Originally developed to ameliorate learning challenges, Edu-K is now used internationally by educators, students, performing artists, athletes and the general public to create positive change and free movement in their lives.

Educational Kinesiology Foundation (International referrals)
Box 3396 Ventura, CA, USA 93006-3396
(800) 356-2109 (805)658-7942
fax: (805) 650-0524 Email: edukfd@aol.com
web: http://www.braingym.com

3-in-1 Concepts (One Brain)

More psychological in its approach, the Three-in-One Concepts model identifies on a conscious, subconscious and body level, the beliefs that have fused into old self-defeating patterns. By consciously identifying and defusing these blocks, "One Brain" facilitates a shift in perception of our relationship with ourselves and the outer world. It allows us to respond to life with clear creative choice.

Three-in-One Concepts (International referrals)
2001 W. Magnolia Blvd. Burbank, CA, USA 91506-1704
phone (818) 841-4786 fax (818) 841-0007

Touch for Health

Touch for Health is a powerful natural healing method that is the foundation upon which the Specialized Kinesiologies in this book are built. Touch for Health has proven itself very effective during the 25 years it has been in use around the world. Using simple muscle testing, TFH shows where stress is locked into the circuits of the body. It identifies and balances these areas using techniques from acupressure, Chinese energy theory and Neurolymphatic massage.

Touch For Health Kinesiology Association of America
11262 Washington Blvd.
Culver City, CA 90230, USA
1(800) 466-8342 or (310) 313-5580
fax (310) 313-9319 web: *http://www.tfh.org*

Canadian Touch for Health Association: See Canadian Association of Specialized Kinesiology

Wellness Kinesiology

Wellness Kinesiology is geared to helping you achieve success and focuses on issues such as weight reduction, self-esteem and habit change. Synthesizing techniques from Touch For Health, other kinesiologies and stress management modalities, it re-educates the body's response to all aspects of stress.

Topping International Institute (International referrals)
2622 Birchwood Avenue #7
Bellingham, WA, U.S.A. 93006-3396
phone & fax (360) 647 2703

General Membership Associations

There are many other kinesiological models beyond the ones I have introduced in this book, some more therapeutic in nature. The membership organizations and learning institutes below can direct you to any of the above, or others that meet your needs.

Canadian Association of Specialized Kinesiology
Box 74508 Kitsilano Postal Unit
Vancouver, BC, CANADA V6K 4P4
(604) 669-8481

International Kinesiology College
Konradstrasse 32
CH-8005 Zurich, SWITZERLAND
41-1-440-42-68   fax 41-1-440-42-69 kinesiology@active.ch

ASK-US Association of Specialized Kinesiologist–US
4201 Wilson Blvd #110-395
Arlington, Virginia, USA 22203-1859
(888) 749-6464

More on the Web:
http://www.kinesiology.net Excellent information on many
  Kinesiologies and international referrals
http://www.touch4health.com   Web page of Dr. John Thie
http://touchpointreflexology.com Good intro to self-care

Brain Based Learning

Exciting, practical applications of the latest brain and educational research for accelerated learning. Vital for teachers, trainers and all who want to learn faster and remember longer.

International Alliance for Learning
1040 South Coast Highway
Encinitas, CA, USA 92024
(800) 426-2989 (760) 634-5146
fax (760) 632-1305

The Brain Store
4202 Sorrento Valley Blvd., Ste. B,
San Diego,CA, USA 92121
(800) 325-4769 (619) 546-7555
fax (619) 546-7560 web: http://www.thebrainstore.com

Enhanced Learning & Integration Inc.

Professional development workshops and certificate training in all the disciplines listed above, including Lightning Learning (see page 174) and facilitator training are just some of the services offered. For general and booking information contact:

Enhanced Learning & Integration Inc.
#713 1489 Marine Drive, West Vancouver, B.C. V7T 1B8
(604) 922-8811 fax: (604) 926-1106
Email: learning@enhancedlearning.com
web: http://www.enhancedlearning.com

ENDNOTES

Section 1: Charting the Course (pages 11-23)

1. Eric Jensen, *Brain-Based 6 Day Certification Manual, page 36.*

2. I refer you to *Brain-Based Learning and Teaching* by Eric Jensen, pp. 120 -121 for a concise summary of brain states, ranging from Delta to Super Beta, and what type of state is best for what type of learning. Jensen also correlates observable physiological signs of the various negative brain states, and the most common strategies used to change states: variations in activities, environment, people, tone, focusing and student input. Changing state can be as simple as a drink of water, a shift in voice, a change in location, lighting or music.

3. Ibid., page 117

4. A brief history of Specialized Kinesiology:
   Applied Kinesiology evolved with medical practitioners who saw the relationship between how muscles and movement can affect and reflect change within the body systems themselves, including brain function. The assessment tool of muscle checking (or testing)––isolating a muscle, and checking its ability to remain locked when stressed—was first used by some medical professionals in the early 1900's. It fell into disuse with the advent of sophisticated technical diagnostic tools. It later became valued by some naturopaths and chiropractors for its natural biofeedback.

   Dr. George Goodheart, a chiropractor who discovered relationships between muscle integrity, functions of the body, and meridian energy, ultimately founded the International College of Applied Kinesiology for medical professionals in the 1960's. Dr. John Thie D.C., a colleague of Dr. Goodheart's, saw the need to share the basic precepts of self care with the layperson. He combined a basic introduction to the buttons and switches of the human body with aspects of oriental meridian theory in his seminal book *Touch For Health*, first published in 1973. This started momentum for a world wide educational model of layman self responsibility that has drawn educators, healing professionals, psychologists and people from all walks of life. Many branches that have sprung from Touch For Health are collectively called Specialized Kinesiology. This book deals with the stress management, educational and performance implications of this field.

5. *Kinesiology,* Ann Holdway, page 11

6. I have patterned my formula on the work of Three In One Concepts who language their model as Event + Perception + Intense emotion = Fusion. Stress Release then is languaged as a "defusion" of the trauma of the past from the current event, allowing a free choice of action in the present, which in turn determines the future.

7. John Varun Maguire, *Become Pain Free with Touch For Health,* p. 9. John generously gave me permission to source his clear explanations on energy switches. This handbook, plus his manual *Maximum Athletic Performance,* are good choices for the person interested in exploring basic Touch For Health concepts.

8. Ibid, p.11

9. Ibid, p.11

10. In conversation with Wayne Topping, PhD.

Section 2: Checking the Equipment (pages 27-38)

1. This behavioral evaluation is adapted with permission from *Basic One Brain* by Gordon Stokes and Daniel Whiteside, Addendum.

2. The Brain Bug is from *Personalized Whole Brain Integration* by Dennison and Dennison, 1985

Section 3: Identifying the Obstacles (pp 41-51)

1. Science News reports 5 minutes talking about something negative raises and maintains cortisol levels which decreases learning & memory for 5 hours. A good reason to control the classic stress response!

2. Dr. Wayne Topping's book, *Success Over Distress* has more information on positively changing personal habits regarding stress. Consult our bibliography for other sources of support.

Section 4: Electromagnetic Balancers (pages 55-61)

1. John Maguire, *Become Pain Free with Touch for Health*, p.11

2. John Thie, Touch For Health p. 17.

3. David Shannahoff-Khalsa, "Breathing Cycle Linked to Hemispheric Dominance." *Brain Mind Bulletin,* Volume 8, Number 3, Jan. 3 , 1983

4. Sheldon Deal, DC, N.M.D.: *Applied Kinesiology Workshop Manual*, New Life Publishing Co., 1973

Section 5: Communication: Brain to Body (pages 65-78)

1. Joel Davis, *Mapping the Brain*, p. 25.

2. This summation was inspired by Gordon Dryden and Jeanette Vos's neat summary in *The Learning Revolution*, p. 108. I have updated and revised their original factoids to my own understanding and purposes. Their work is a good book choice for an introduction to accelerated learning.

3. Ron Van der Meer and Ad Dudink, *The Brain Pack,* "The Chemistry of Nerve Impulses" section. This absolutely delightful pop-out book epitomizes brain compatible learning, with the activation of almost all the multiple intelligences and senses for learning. The only thing missing is actual smell. (See next footnote for more on multiple intelligences) Pictures, text, activity, sound, touch, interaction in all three dimensions! A welcome addition to any library.

4. From the basic concept of intelligence being either "You are" or "You're not", based upon traditional school performance and the three R's, the educational community has moved into an awareness of Multiple Intelligences or giftedness. First popularized by Dr. John Gardner, his original theory of 7 intelligences included: Verbal/linguistic, logical/mathematical, visual/spatial, bodily/kinesthetic, musical/rhythmic, interpersonal and intrapersonal. The definition of specific intelligences has since expanded, with some researchers claiming there are potentially thousands. The bottom line is that the more learning is presented in a way that stimulates different processing centers of the brain, the more impact, the easier and more deeply layered is the learning. My Lightning Learning workshop explores the practical applications of this and other brain based principles. Eric Jensen's *Brain Compatible Strategies* is a good quick start to building brain compatible techniques into teaching and learning.

5. Eric Jensen, *The Learning Brain*, page 48.

6. Robert Sylwester, *A Celebration of Neurons* p. 41.

7. Russell L. Blaylock, M.D., *Excitotoxins: The Taste that Kills*, page 10.

8. *To support your back brain*: Reinforce a sense of security, establish positive and purposeful ritual, provide transition time between tasks, stretch, relax and discuss. Support suggestions from Eric Jensen, *Brain Based Learning and Teaching*

9. *To support your midbrain:* The midbrain responds to safety, relaxation and grounding. Emotions, active discussion, roleplay and debates, music and storytelling, games, and theater all support the mid-brain, and help imprint long term memory. Support suggestions from Eric Jensen, *Brain Based Learning and Teaching*.

10. Carla Hannaford, *Smart Moves*, pp. 31& 89

11. *To support your Cerebral Cortex:* The cerebral cortex looks for associations and patterns. It responds to novelty, sensory stimulation of all kinds, color, mind maps, field trips, varying eye patterns, pre-exposure to material to provide a framework for learning. Support suggestions from Eric Jensen, *Brain Based Learning and Teaching.*

12. These concepts truly live at the heart of Educational Kinesiology. For a more in-depth exploration of support for the three dimensions I refer you to a course in Brain Gym. See page 62 for a referral to the Educational Kinesiology Foundation for more information.

13. Marilee Boitson, in conversation, pointed out the obvious truth that developmentally it is random and reflex body movement that underpins the layering of the neural connections that ultimately become the sophisticated circuitry enabling conscious, brain ordered, intentional movement.

Section 6: Emotional Balancers (pages 81-89)

1. Sourced from Antonio R. Damasio, *Descartes' Error*, as referenced in Hannaford, Carla, *Smart Moves* page 52.

2. Ron Van der Meer and Ad Dudink, *The Brain Pack*, Emotion section.

3. I strongly recommend Candace Pert's book *Molecules of Emotion*. The discoverer of the opiate receptor, and a respected neuroscientist, Pert's life work is very supportive of mind/body approaches to emotional work. She also gives a fascinating insider's look at the role of women in science and the fiercely competitive and ruthless "publish or perish" politics in the scientific community.

4. Antonio Domasio, Descartes' Error, p. 144.

5. Robert Sylwester, *A Celebration of Neurons*, p. 45.

6. I invite you to investigate three basic internationally available branches of specialized kinesiology, and should you choose, their offshoots. Educational Kinesiology provides a gentle system of re-education with Brain Gym® and other non intrusive processes, and is a superb choice for those who prefer re-education through movement. For those who would like a more psychological look at their emotional triggers and the "story" that is locked into their emotional responses, I can suggest you experience the insightful work of Three In One Concepts. For those who are most comfortable with a more physical approach, Touch For Health provides a superb layman's introduction to restoring well-being and integrity to the hu-

man body. For information on how to contact these and other organizations see pp 162-164.

7. I refer you to the reference section of *Molecules of Emotion* by Candace Pert, for a wonderful synthesis of other mind/body disciplines which may prove of interest to you.

Section 7: Communication: Body to Brain (pages 93-98)

1. *The Brain Pack*, Ron Van der Meer and Ad Dudink, Emotions section; Blowing Your Top and Cooling Off.

2. Candace Pert, *Molecules of Emotion*. pp. 26-27

3. Ibid, pp. 139-140.

4. Pert's research supports her thesis that "Neuropeptides and their receptors join the brain, glands, and immune system in a network of communication between brain and body, probably representing the biochemical substrata of emotion" (Pert & Ruff, Journal of Immunology ,1985, as quoted in *Molecules of Emotion*. p.178) It seems safe to assume that this chemical information system is at work during the classic stress response, triggering the physiological changes to the endocrine, digestive, respiratory, cardiovascular, and immune systems, both a result of, and a cause of the change in emotional experience.

5. Richard S. Snell, MD, PhD, *Clinical Neuroanatomy for Medical Students*, Little, Brown & Co. Inc., Boston, 1980, pp. 66, 67, 69.

6. Robert Sylwester, *A Celebration of Neurons*, p.69

7. You can also choose to seek out an electrodermal screening practitioner who uses High Tech Biofeedback to check the system.

Section 8: Brain/Body Balancers (pages 101-111)

1. Janet Goodrich, *Natural Vision Improvement*, page 31.

Section 9: Sharpening your Senses (p 115-127)

1. Steve Parker, *The Human Body* p.94 Chemosenses

2. Robert Sylwester, *Celebration of Neurons*, p.66

3. Carla Hannaford, *Advanced Physiology of Brain Gym* Course

4. Called Lazy 8s™ in Brain Gym, this activity has been highly refined for many applications in Brain Gym and Vision Gym. See Lazy 8s for Writing, page 133, and Alphabet 8s, page 133, for other applications of this activity.

5. Robert Sylwester, *A Celebration of Neurons*, p.49

6. Carla Hannaford, *Smart Moves*. page 35

Section 10: Fine Motor (pages 131-134)

1. Rita Edwards, P.R.E.P.A.R.E. Writing Program, information available through the Educational Kinesiology Foundation

Section 11: Real Life: How to apply what you've learned (pages 137-158)

1. Willingness to Benefit was sourced from the Three in One Concepts balancing procedure.

2. Those who choose to explore Brain Gym will experience a wonderful five step Action Balance process. I refer you to the *Brain Gym Handbook, The Student Guide to Brain Gym* p.10. for Brain Gym's 5 Steps to Easy Learning. My interpretation of the change process resonates strongly with Paul and Gail Dennison's original approach.

3. I first sourced and adapted the concept of S.M.A.R.T. goal setting from Dr. Wayne Topping, who in turn credits Charles Givens in his book *Super Self*.

BIBLIOGRAPHY AND RECOMMENDED MATERIAL

* indicates a good introductory choice

Armstrong, Thomas, *7 Kinds of Smart,* Plume, Penguin Books, New York, NY, 1993

Barhydt, Hap PhD. & Elizabeth Barhydt: *Self Help for Stress and Pain.* Loving Life, 1989 Available through Touch For Health Kinesiology Association of America

Barrett, Susan L.: *It's All in your Head.* Free Spirit Publishing Inc., Minneapolis, MN, 1992

Begley, Sharon: "How to Build a Baby's Brain," *Newsweek Magazine.* Special Edition Your Child Spring/Summer New York, NY, 1997

Blaylock, Russell L. M.D.: *Excitotoxins; The Taste that Kills.* Health Press, Santa Fe, NM, 1994

Bryan, Jenny: *Your Amazing Brain.* Joshua Morris Publishing Inc., Westport, CT, 1995

Bruun, Ruth Dowling, M. D. & Bertel Bruun, M. D.: *The Human Body.* Random House, New York, NY, 1982

Buzan, Tony and Barry Buzan: *The Mind Map Book.* BBC Books, London, 1993

Chopra, Deepak M.D.: *Quantum Healing: Exploring the Frontiers of Mind/Body Medicine.* Bantam Books, New York, NY, 1989

Cole, Jan: *Re-Pattern Your Sabotaging Ways.* 1985 available through Touch for Health Kinesiology Association of America.

Damasio, Antonio R.: *Descartes' Error: Emotion, Reason, and the Human Brain.* Avon, New York, NY, 1995

Davis, Joel: *Mapping the Mind: The Secrets of the Human Brain & How it Works.* Carol Publishing Group, Secaucus, NJ, 1997

Deal, Sheldon, DC, N.M.D.: Applied *Kinesiology Workshop Manual,* New Life Publishing Co., 1001 N. Swan Rd., Tucson, Ariz. 85711, 1973

de Bono, Edward: *Serious Creativity.* Harper Collins, Toronto, Canada, 1992

Dennison, Paul E., PhD., Gail E. Dennison and J. D. Teplitz, PhD: *Brain Gym for Business.* Edu-Kinesthetics Inc. Ventura, CA, 1994

Dennison, Paul E. PhD & Gail E. Dennison: *Brain Gym Handbook* . Edu-Kinesthetics Inc., Ventura, CA, 1989

* Dennison, Paul E. PhD & Gail E. Dennison: *Brain Gym Teacher's Edition.* Edu-Kinesthetics Inc., Ventura, CA, 1989

Dennison, Paul E. PhD: "The Physical Aspect of Brain Organization" *Brain Gym Journal* Vol. 10 No. 3. December 1996

Dennison, Paul E. PhD & Gail E. Dennison: *Switching On.* Edu-Kinesthetics Inc., Ventura, CA, 1981

De Porter, Bobbie with Mike Kernacki: *Quantum Business.* Dell Publishing, New York, NY, 1997

* De Porter, Bobbie: *Quantum Learning.* Dell Publishing, New York, NY, 1992

Dryden, Gordon and Jeanette Vos, Ed. D.: *The Learning Revolution.* Jalmar Press, Rolling Hills Estates, CA, 1994

Gardner, Howard: *Frames of Mind: The Theory of Multiple Intelligences.* Basic Books, New York, NY, 1985

Gerber, Richard, M.D.: *Vibrational Medicine.* New Choices for Healing Ourselves. Bear & Company, Santa Fe, NM., 1988

Goodrich, Janet: *Natural Vision Improvement.* Celestial Arts, Berkeley, CA, 1986

* Hannaford, Carla, PhD: *Smart Moves: Why Learning Is Not All In Your Head.* Great Ocean Publishers, Arlington, VA, 1995

Hannaford, Carla, PhD: *The Dominance Factor.* Great Ocean Publishers, Arlington, VA, 1997

*Holdway, Ann: *Kinesiology; Muscle Testing and Energy Balancing for Health and Wellbeing.* Element, Inc., Rockport, MA, 1995

Howard, Pierce J.: *The Owner's Manual for the Brain.* Leornian Press, Austin, TX, 1994

Jensen, Eric: *Brain Based Learning & Teaching: Turning* Point Publishing, Hauppauge, New York, NY, 1995

* Jensen, Eric: *Brain Compatible Strategies.* Turning Point Publishing, Del Mar, CA 1997

Jensen, Eric: *Completing the Puzzle.* Turning Point Publishing, Hauppauge, New York, NY, 1996

* Jensen, Eric: *Student Success Secrets.* Turning Point Publishing, Hauppauge, New York, NY, 1993

Jensen, Eric: *The Learning Brain.* Turning Point Publishing, San Diego CA, 1994

Kapit, Wynn and Lawrence M. Elson: *The Anatomy Coloring Book.* Harper & Row, New York, NY, 1977

Kotaluk, Ronald: *Inside the Brain, Revolutionary Discoveries of How the Mind Works.* Andrews Mcmeel Publishing, Kansas City , MI, 1996,1997

LeDoux, Joseph: *The Emotional Brain: The Mysterious Underpinnings of Emotional Life.* Simon & Schuster, New York, N.Y. , 1996

Maguire, John: *Become Pain Free With Touch For Health,* Kinesiology Institute, Malibu, CA 1996. 1(800) 501-4878 or (310) 457-8407

Mathers, Douglas: *You and Your Body: Brain.* Troll Associates, Eagle Books Ltd., 1992

* Miller, Jonathan: *The Human Body.* Viking Penguin, New York, NY, 1983

Nash, Madeleine J.: "Fertile Minds," *Time Magazine.* Canadian Edition, June 9, 1997

Noonan, David: *Neuro–Life on the Frontlines of Brain Surgery and Neurological Medicine.* Simon & Schuster, New York, NY, 1989

*Parker, Steve: *How the Body Works.* Reader's Digest, Pleasantville, NY 1994

*Parker, Steve: *Brain Surgery for Beginners and Other Major Operations for Minors.* The Millbrook Press, Brookfield, CN, 1993

*Pert, Candace, PhD: *Molecules of Emotion.* Scribner, New York, NY 1997

*Promislow, Sharon: *The Top Ten Stress Releasers.* Enhanced Learning & Integration Inc, West Vancouver, Can. 1994

*Sacks, Oliver: *An Anthropologist on Mars.* Random House Inc,. New York. 1995

Sher, Barbara and Gottlieb, Annie: *Wishcraft: How to Get What You Really Want.* Ballantine Books, New York, NY, 1979

Stokes, Gordon and Daniel Whiteside: *One Brain: Dyslexic Learning Correction and Brain Integration.* Three in One Concepts, Burbank, CA, 1984

* Stokes, Gordon and Daniel Whiteside: *Tools of the Trade.* Three In One Concepts, Burbank, CA, 1996

Sunbeck, Deborah PhD: *Infinity Walk; Preparing your mind to learn.* Jalmar Press, Torrence, CA, 1996

Suzuki, David: "The Brain: Our Universe Within" The Discovery Channel, 1994

Swerdlow, Joel L.: "Quiet Miracles of the Brain" *National Geographic.* Washington, DC, Vol. 187, No. 6, June 1995

* Sylwester, Robert: *A Celebration of Neurons.* Association for Supervision and Curriculum Development, Alexandria, VA, 1995

Teplitz, Jerry PhD: *Switched On Living.* Hampton Roads Publishing Co. Inc., Norfolk, VA, 1994

* Thie, John, DC: *Touch for Health.* DeVorss & Company, Marina de Rey, CA, 1973,1994

Topping, Wayne, PhD: *Stress Release.* Topping International Institute, Bellingham, WA, 1985

* Topping, Wayne PhD: *Success Over Distress.* Topping International Institute, Bellingham, WA, 1990

* Van der Meer, Ron and Ad Dudink: The *Brain Pack.* Running Press, Philadelphia, PA, 1996

INDEX

PREVIEW OF COMING ATTRACTIONS

Attach an emotion: Always ask "How will this make a difference to me?"

Manage your state with Brain/Body Balancers

Use appropriate music as you read: baroque is best

Chunk the new learning: 20 minutes tops, then review

Bright, natural light

Use color & mind mapping, for note making

Keep room cool

Provide challenge and novelty: set goals

Use your multiple intelligences

Take frequent breaks: for fruit or a stretch

USE THESE EASY STRATEGIES TO GET MORE OUT OF YOUR TIME WITH THIS BOOK

Currently only available as a live workshop with Sharon Promislow. Call Enhanced Learning for booking information. Book, audiotapes and video coming soon!

Electrify your brain and your learning with dramatic discoveries on how the human brain learns best. Having improved your brain/body "hardware" with the stress and state management techniques presented in *Making the Brain /Body Connection*, your next step is to acquire the leading edge learning 'software"—the latest accelerated, brain-friendly" learning strategies. You will discover:

• How you can learn faster, retain information longer, and have more fun in the process!

• How to create an optimal environment and state for success working with the brain's natural cycles, rhythms and chemistry.

• Productivity enhancing skill sets for everything from note-taking, rapid reading to memory strategies.

• How to effortlessly improve seeing, hearing, memory attention and writing

• How you uniquely learn best, and how to switch on your multiple intelligences.

PRODUCTS & SERVICES

Name: _____

Address: _____

City:_____ Prov/State:_____

Country_____ Zipcode:_____

Phone _____ Email _____

	Putting Out the Fire of Fear (238 pages)	$14.95 ea.	
	Making the Brain/Body Connection (176 pages)	$15.95 ea.	
	The Top Ten Stress Releasers (36 pages)	$ 9.00 ea.	
	The Top Ten Stress Releasers (Pad of 100)	$12.00 ea.	
	The Top Ten Brain/Body Integrators Pad (Pad of 100)	$12.00 ea.	
	Biodots- pkg of 10 (includes shipping)	$5.95 ea.	
	Biodots- pkg of 100 (includes shipping	$12.95 ea.	
	Send me information on Enhanced Learning speakers	FREE	
	Send me a complete product and price list	FREE	
Please add $4.00 Shipping and Handling for the first item and $1.00 for each additional item		**$4.00**	
Canadian residents add 7% GST			
Total in US dollars			

Send check or money order payable to Enhanced Learning & Integration Inc.

NO C.O.D • Prices subject to change, call for quantity discount • All prices in $US

❑ Visa ❑ Mastercard #_____

Expiration Date _____/_____ Signature: _____

ENHANCED LEARNING & INTEGRATION INC
#1401 1238 Seymour Street, Vancouver, B.C. V6B 6J3
Telephone: (604) 682-8192 Fax: (604) 696-6276 Email: sales@enhancedlearning.com
http://www.enhancedlearning.com

SHARON PROMISLOW

A popular international speaker in the corporate and educational sectors, Sharon is a Specialized Kinesiologist certified in Educational Kinesiology (Brain Gym®), Touch for Health, Three In One Concepts, Stress Release and Brain Based Learning.

Sharon facilitates innovative professional and personal development workshops on Stress Management, Brain/Body Integration, Creativity, Reading, Memory, Teaching and Presentation Skills.

Sharon's background includes postgraduate studies in English Literature and Psychology. She was a communications consultant before being drawn to the field of Specialized Kinesiology by her fascination with new brain/body research and breakthroughs in learning and performance enhancement.

She is also the author of *Putting Out the Fire of Fear, The Top Ten Stress Releasers*, and *The Top Ten Brain/Body Integrators*. She co-authored *Screen Test—How to Screen for Sensitivities in Your Diet and Environment*, and has designed a line of presentation materials for professional speakers.

Sharon was a founder of the Canadian Association of Specialized Kinesiology. She is President of Enhanced Learning & Integration, Inc. in Vancouver, British Columbia, Canada, where she resides with her family.

CATHRINE LEVAN

A former world champion kick boxer, Cathrine brings focused energy and an "It's easy—anyone can do it!" attitude to everything she takes on—from designing clothing to driving a backhoe. Unveiling her artistic talent in this book is just one more facet for this multi-talented marketing director and product development consultant.

A trained Specialized Kinesiologist herself, Cathrine is a past president of the Canadian Association of Specialized Kinesiology. She has many interests and can often be found scouring computer manuals, shooting at the range, creating art boards, playing chess or hiking through BC's rugged mountains.